Across the Layers

Albert Goldbarth

ACROSS THE LAYERS

Poems Old and New

The University of Georgia Press

Athens and London

© 1993 by Albert Goldbarth
All rights reserved
Published by the University of Georgia Press
Athens, Georgia 30602

Designed by Betty Palmer McDaniel
Set in ten on thirteen Sabon
by Tseng Information Systems, Inc.
Printed and bound by Thomson-Shore, Inc.
The paper in this book meets the guidelines for
permanence and durability of the Committee on
Production Guidelines for Book Longevity of the
Council on Library Resources.

Printed in the United States of America
97 96 95 94 93   C 5   4   3   2   1
97 96 95 94 93   P 5   4   3   2   1

Library of Congress Cataloging in Publication Data
Goldbarth, Albert.
    [Poems. Selections]
    Across the layers : poems old and new / Albert Goldbarth.
        p.   cm.
    ISBN 0-8203-1547-8 (alk. paper).
    — ISBN 0-8203-1548-6 (pbk. :   alk. paper)
    I. Title.
    PS3557.O354A64   1993
    811'.54—dc20   92-38270

British Library Cataloging in Publication Data available

    Poems are reprinted from the following books: *Different Fleshes* (Hobart and William Smith Colleges Press, 1979); *Faith* (New Rivers Press, 1981); *Original Light* (Ontario Review Press, 1983); *Arts & Sciences* (Ontario Review Press, 1986); *Popular Culture* (Ohio State University Press, 1989); *Heaven and Earth* (University of Georgia Press, 1991). Of the new material, "Dual" originally appeared in the *Georgia Review* and "Gallery" in the *Ontario Review*. My very appreciative thanks to the editors and publishers involved.

    Earlier work appears as originally published. The poems of the sequence "The Central Light" are arranged for theme and narrative, not by chronology of composition or publication.

For Irving Goldbarth

> *. . . across the layers of shale,*
> *worm-warren, and motherlode coal that separate us*

("The Dynamics of Huh")

Contents

Introduction

When *Different Fleshes* was first published in 1979, I subtitled it, after conferring with my editor, "a novel-poem." It follows the adventures and transformations of Vander Clyde of Round Rock, Texas (follows them intermittently, sidelooping into numerous other lives and times and places) in an alternation of prose and poetry, narrative and lyricism. In a way, the piece is *about* these kinds of balances, and especially about the idea that the journey to remake one's self can be an outward travel (for instance, expatriatism) or inward, psychic pilgrimage; and that these equal but "different fleshes" can find a link of conjoining.

Among the busy background citizenry of this booklength work is a father "in the brick house / on Washtenaw Avenue," and the second, the middle, section of *Across the Layers*, "The Central Light," allows him to assume, in this light, a central position. These twenty-two pieces range from poems first published in book form in 1981 to new poems never yet in a book. And I hope, as well, that they range interestingly in strategy and approach, and so provide a varied surface as they go about, below that skin, their mutual exploration of filial memory and elegy.

Finally, "Dual"—a latest example of what I continue to call an "essay-poem." The father figure reappears, the filial gestures culminate; and I'd like to think that the father and the piece's other presence, the photographer Diane Arbus (whose portraits so strikingly capture "different fleshes" of endless sorts), exemplify, as the title implies, notions of duality that well extend the thematic concerns of the "novel-poem" from fourteen years before.

When Karen Orchard of the University of Georgia Press first suggested the possibility of a volume that collected old poems and new, I was immediately grateful, not only for the chance to revivify out-of-print work (for example, *Different Fleshes* disappeared about as soon as its first reviews were printed, its publisher having flared as brightly—yet briefly—as a meteor) but also for the saving opportunity to place some poems of many years' creation into what seemed, at last, to be their most fitting continuum.

This isn't, then, a standard "new and selected poems": many of my early books and chapbooks are not represented. But the poems included do span, in their composition, fifteen years or more; and I hope they exist now (strictly, "reexist," for some of them) in a proper simultaneity presided over by, as *Different Fleshes* says, the "moon we / sigh over, and then write, / write poems under."

DIFFERENT FLESHES

a novel-poem

first

He was always covered in dirt, and tan—the dirt the topmost smudge of the cattlecorn, cedar, and pecan lengths of central Texas. And so his skin *was* Round Rock, Texas: sun, hitting soil. He was seven. Born in 1904. What we know:

of his father, nothing.

of his brothers and / or sisters (if any), nothing.

of his mother, owned a millinery shop in Round Rock, in summer the flat white bolts of cloth in the window discolored under the sun, so never sold, "She was artistic, very much admired culture," and once in the August sky like a kiln, in the sky like a limeworks, she took him to Austin "40¢ and Roundtrip 75¢" to the circus.

—Vander, Vander, Goosey Gander!

Nothing

—Hey Vander, Hey Vander, Hey Dumb Goosey Gander!

Nothing

—Hey Vander cantcha hear or nothin!

(quiet) Lee' me lone

—Hey you been pickin cotton Vander Gander wit th darkies agin (hit)

Nothing

—(hit)

(quiet) Lee' me lone Hey!

—(hit) (blood)

pouring it out, then falling in it, and waiting and then long after the laughing goes its own way: watching it turn gelid, rolling balls the size of rabbit droppings from this his noseblood and Texas dust

Of Round Rock in 1904:

You rode in over the wooden bridge. At the intersection of Brushy Creek and the Chisolm Trail. The Rock itself was under the bridge, and twenty-six years earlier: Sam Bass the desperado "Robin Hood on a Fast Horse" entered the bridge with his own blood the taste of a bullet souring on his tongue, rode in to Round Rock, Texas, to die: four drugstores, four lumber yards, one bakery, six hotels, 1,500 people. He'd terrorized the vicinity. Now, late afternoon, the loss of blood, the sun, had turned him nearly to butcher's produce slung on a sorrel mare. She took the bridge slow, her hoofs making U's on the wood slats with the careful procedure of grade-school penmanship. U's of hollow sound. By the time her heaving belly passed over the Rock, she was shaking off flies from her flanks with the specially iridescent fleshtwitch of horse, but they landed on Bass and his labored breathing wasn't enough to dislodge them. Those stories about his last hours . . . ! And then was buried: four slabs of stone about waist-high. By 1904:

the Round Rock Creamery, where they brought in their milk to skim, was starting to fail (and later busted completely, not having refrigeration)

a broom from the Broom Factory was entered in the 1904 World's Fair in St. Louis, Missouri, "and won a gold medal" (the factory closed down in 1919)

the bridge still stood (it would wash out in 1913 / though be rebuilt)

at the Southern Presbyterian Institute Public School, he balanced his teeth on his teeth like cornerstones being laid for his life, he put the whole of him in his hand, and practiced: UUUUUUU

—Very good, Vander Clyde

He wanted anything but seven, anything but Round Rock.

His hand doing U's with the delicate arabesque of lace. The Rock beneath the bridge, its one continuous thrash of the fast black water: into a doily.

And sun the sun.

That Sam Bass, there was a man's own man. The other children played at Sam Bass. —And I'm gon shoot you, Vander! (hit) Hey lookit him run! (how he could run)

Bending for the cotton, with the field hands. They called them "hands." And they bent, so from an immaculate distance their backs like a piano's hammers some well-washed lavendered hands played.

He looked at his hands. He could dance the rows in the fields.

—Vander, Vander, Salamander!

But he could dance the rows. The white trash backs, the black backs: keys. A piano. He heard in his head when he picked. He danced little U's for the sun.

The way they did that one time at the circus.

He was seven, he was Vander Clyde, and what do you do when your heart that you'll have to bring with always, the pump of you, is Round Rock?

He was right in the extremes.

The rest was all wrong, and he knew it. The skinny chest they hit. The po'boy's ribby bellyskin in the loam in the sun, in the unction, of central Texas. Heart, the middle of him.

—Hey Vander, Vander, Gotcher Dander!

oh look at my feet (on the long black-umber dirt between cotton) oh look at my hands (like birds around him, like two birds in the sun) oh listen (a drum: I don't know from where, but a drum) I can do . . . (to pick out a pebble, that one there, and close your eyes, and leap, to let your eyes be in your feet) . . . this! (and land a perfect cairn of seven-year-boy on a pebble, all the while an aviary around) my hands my birds (not losing your balance once) and I can do it with *that* pebble waaaay over there, oh listen (the drum from the circus) and that one (perfect: his hands) and that one (his toes where the blood did ten red U's and turned around back) oh look (his extremes, the right parts of him, and they would take him, rightly, into extremity, so that by 1923 he . . .) and that one and that one and that one and

—Vander Clyde, damn you, you picks aw you gets on home

By the '20s, they'd all left home. He was
here, it was morning, the Seine all rinds
on fire, yes and his skin like the bookstalls
along the embankment was ready to open and
be browsed—Hemingway
of course; but so what? The point is, when
in that cafe on the Place St-Michel, he tilted a
half-carafe of its dry white wine to the petulant
Paris sky, and let its light carry everything
of the ragpatch artists' quarter, of a spot
off the Quai where men with cane poles and quill floats
fished for *goujon,* of the Arc and of the Tuileries
                                                onto his page; or
when, after, he drank the dozen seapools straight
from his blueplate of oysters, and let one piquant
bead of it stay on the table, among his shavings,
to focus something of sun as a crystal ball did the future;
                                                        then
through that special expatriate
clarity: he saw Michigan "and
since it was a wild, cold, blowing day
it was that sort of day in the story."
He sat there, poor, with Joyce in his pocket
on loan. The wine was strong and attenuated, almost
a note beyond human range, and
as an *aperitif* noon came close, in the back of his eyes a
snaggle of Michigan pine made black-and-cream
serration against Ann Arbor clouds.
                                Joyce
looked up; his one eye
weary. All day, so far, that look had been the only
knowing container of Jesuit /
pubdrunk / downonyourknees / deepKellygreen / and wake's-keen
Ireland in all of France, and now

8

the eye hurt, and was heavy, and had to be carried
with a kind of deliberate grace
into the Metro.
                              Pound looked up;
he'd brought the subway home, to the studio on rue
Notre-Dames-des-Champs; now with the whole of what
he'd saved by heart from Idaho, Pennsylvania,
Trieste, and London, he needed to keep that
long dark tube the same but
change it—Imagism. (Monet
                              and a tube of black paint). Before
the world grayed over completely this afternoon, she
brought her tugboat body home to 27
rue de Fleurus, in tow every
hare's-blood and goat's-milk scent
from the market—Stein. She'd studied under
one of the Jameses—William—but now it was Paris,
Paris, Paris, old clothes (Hemingway called them
"steerage clothes") and her language in new skin; so
she bent again to words—*The Making
of Americans* (Hemingway: "unbelievably long")—while
Alice took a blade to the four fur socks they
leave on a hare. Near
dinner, one of the Jameses
—Henry—touched the woman inside him, oh like an
on button, and he wrote too. Really more
anguished, and more rarified, than that; but I mean as
Stein took her butcherblock-shape of a hand
to the man part in her, and rummaged, so in that
same Paris hour of spiritual synchronicity, many
gestures, out of many hurts, made dazzle.
                              (Monet:
"When it gets dark," he once said,
"I feel as though I'm dying." Then his eyes, a little
like Joyce's, went dark. And from his twisted
tubes, his pigments: water lilies.
Radiant and fierce). And this isn't
even mentioning Scott Fitzgerald. You think I'm

name-dropping. Yes, well . . . there they were,
at Sylvia Beach's English-language bookstore 12
rue de l'Odeon, on the shelves, or looking at the shelves,
and wanting a place there, sometimes
seizing on a single American word, a word
of mothertongue, and carrying it
at the back of the *lingua franca,* rolling it over
all night like a pebble
with on a journey for something . . . it kept the mouth
wet, working. He looked up
—Hemingway. And closed his notebook. Hadley
would be waiting, with the small stick fire,
chestnuts, mmm and that way a fresh, hard French towel
reddened her breasts. If the story were good,
if it sold . . . or maybe he'd do a stint reporting,
he'd see. The Seine was a dark tube ("transplanting,"
he wrote, "could be as necessary with people as with
other growing things") and Hemingway walked home.
"Home?" Yes. It
was 1923, Monet looked up. It was 1878. And
he was a man on the Seine,
in a white smock, looking, in a skiff. The tubes of color were something
new—having come on the market just in 1861. A
citron ruff of light on the water—then even that
began to fade. The brush
responded—heavy paint, sombre, the stable
Seine: that great, slow, settled
heart of his city. But this was Monet. So then
the bright broken
crimsons in craze on the skin of the water!

Vander Clyde?

He looked up. Dead night.

—Yes maam?

—Just wanted to see if you was awake yet.

Her pause. A cricket somewhere far: the only oiled motor turning in this baked black Round Rock emptiness. Chrrr.

—(nothing)

—I know it gets lonely here sometime. (what we know: of her husband: if she ever had a "husband": nothing) There's just us two.

—Yes maam.

A millinery shop. Her white dress in his black room in the deeper bituminous blackness of Round Rock. Hem a black wave's fanned foam.

—It was hard for you today in them fields, wasn't it?

—(nothing / then:) Yeah.

—I know, it was hard in the shop. A dummy came undone, a sample tipped over, oh.

Just that: oh. It filled the room on her lavender. That was the world.

Outside, somewhere, all black, and hidden in black, like hairs in a nostril, in a darky-man's nostril, outside: the pitch in the poor folks' cabins was black, and fit in its wood cracks like uneasy having of sex. 8,000 bales at the cotton yard, in black wire—almost mercator-lines, they were so tight. Vander Clyde swallowed. A hog by its hind legs—swinging leisurely in hot black breeze, in stink. And a curried mare at W. J. Fouse's Livery and Feed Stable letting the two isosceles blacknesses deep in her pricked ears fill: chrrr. black Round black Rock, it was night.

Her white dress a cream on top. Her white dress you could fall in forever.

—Look, pardner, smile. Next week sometime . . .

She sat on the edge of his bed. He was seven, he wanted anything but. The hot and dirt of the day still in his pores, a tattoo, it wouldn't wash. No matter the tin tub and scrubbing with the horse brush even. Round Rock forever.

—. . . we'll go to the circus again, in Austin.

How she said it, on her lavender. The way she said her dress was imported from Paris, each word separate with a little glow inside like lightningbugs, something against the dark. When she hugged him, so white, it was something he shouldn't ever feel, he knew—like the sky bent down, with substance, and showing you something on its other side that really should have been saved. Dress white as a cloud listing over, dress-pressing-him-clean.

—G'night maam.

—When is it ever, child? (pause . then:) Sweet sleep, Vander Clyde.

He gets up at night.

Imported. From. Paris.

In her dress, he gets up, her bodice the lace of the very angels' mantillas, the network of white web holding together a tangerine, milk, her immaculate silks in the darkness, her dress, he gets up, a pastel, a satin, her skirts: an extreme white bell, oh her dress in its fineness and clemency.

It was 1911. By 1923 he

1878:

(In Paris, Monet completes *The Banks of the Seine*. That river's leaning trees, and grassy sides, and /distant/ housetops: given, by him, the flow of water. Everything: watermovement waterface. How the river's *there*, unavoidable, in place—but changes. Go to paint it x, by the time your brush maneuvers /no matter how quick/ it's x-prime. Not that this worries Monet: you see him?, there, a man like a gaudy cork float in the bobbing of daylight . . . one more flicker, he needs one more red flicker . . . It's:)

morning

again in /sigh/ a small central Texas town

not far from Round Rock really. One dun street, its facing rows of dun storefronts and, at even this early, many dun faces among the troughs and hitched horses. This is what happened:

A bucket-jawed 'poke chawed tabaccer in front of Dan's Blacksmith (& Hardware & Hostelry). An overdressed lady in lavender gloves and a wimple-sized bonnet hobbled toward the Merchantmens & Cattlemens First Bank. The horses' shadows, sober and blocky in A.M. sun, lay with the presence of so many steamer-trunks; a stevedore wouldn't want to heft those shadows, not in the coming noon heat. And the dogbark /sigh/ and the flybuzz /sigh/ and a kid in dun suspenders rolling a barrelhoop still crusted with brine on its inside, Mrs. Lavender Gloves reached the door, an ice wagon trundled by, the tabaccer was spat, Mrs. Lavender Gloves with a dainty move took her hat off,

"Hands up or I blast you to h--l!"
—Sam Bass.
Rode off with three men and eight moneybags.

"D--n, we was robbed by Sam Bass himself. That was Sam Bass."
"I'll be. You sure?"
"He had *me* fooled in that getup. Wait'll I tell . . . Sam Bass!" Again, as if repetition made truer: "Sam Bass!"
"He's a man in a hunnerd."

✳.

riding out crazy on top of it all, like crestfleck, feeling the moneybags
bang on the turns, the whole slow wide-eyed territory galloped through in
shock, adrenalin and victory, flinging the gloves to the wind let them slap
the face of the sky for a challenge I'm Sam Bass boys and I do not take no
bullchip talk from nobody no sir and

one day in 1878 something like this happened: "Hands up or I blast you to/

pain, in his back, more surprise than pain, it's pain in a place of muscles
that never declared themselves before, a kind of surprise, of disappoint-
ment, in the world / on his mare like a side of beef, almost smudging the
air in passage / if I can make it over the bridge / another rider on his horse,
along with him, no wonder the mare's so slow, who is it, oh it's Heat, it's
Mr. Heat, no wonder / just over the bridge, that's all, to the cool end /
over the bridge

over the Round Rock

and into town. ". . . it is agin my profession to blow on my pals. If
a man knows anything, he ought to die with it in him." (this,
according to Charles L. Martin's account)

he made it over the bridge
he died with it in him
his last words, according to Martin: "The world is bobbing around me!"
(So
        Monet
one day in 1878, smiles: here, a
final red flicker,
good! Oh dun for the
base, the Seine, but its surface: extremity's
faceted dazzle. Watermotion,
waterflesh, life bobbing. Turns
to brush fresh canvas. And paints
till sunset closes
color down for the night.)

*

"The bridge was dismantled during World War II and the metal supports used in the scrap metal drives." (—Round Rock Kiwanis Club)

*

So many names, so many years . . .
It's dark now.
—Sweet sleep, Vander Clyde. Say your prayers.

Where the snake will slough its skin
/In that place let me begin

Where the deer will drop its horn
/In that place let me be born

Where the man will change his face
/Let me waken in that place

Even before the idea of desk, of lamp: the moon
was a desklamp. This is because before
the idea of poems, we wrote poems. Before the slaver-,
shagend-, hunker- and howl-
beasts lifted themselves on two feet into
my fathers, my fathers
wrote poems. In the crackle of ancestor-plasm,
with twig and with cockbone, by matriarch-gel,
they wrote. Their whole world, a first draft. Before
my father wrote poems, in the brick house
on Washtenaw Avenue, there
in the old days before they tore up Humboldt Park, he
washed sleep's crumbs from his eyes. The night
was full of many mistakes. But
now it was morning; clouds were smudged
like artgum, having erased an error. They
took the gray, my father dried his hands.
My mother hummed. I was in the future.
I was a bell, the day was still a delicate spiderwebbing
over the mouth of that bell. Outside, the planet
wrote poems. A peacock broke protein
into its fan like a prism breaking light.
A man's lip split up blood, in an alley, behind
the picketline, dark. She hummed and my father
returned from work and one night
a bell rang. He said "I knew it, here, I predicted
it in a poem. Albert." After
his father. My mother fed the bird, the seeds
no bigger than sleep rubbed every morning from her eyes.
I remember. We wrote poems. The planet turned
upside-down but Washtenaw never suffered.
Sometimes I heard them, behind the door, a *skreek*
like car parts, a rousing the air as of wings.
So many years later I would quote that
poem, and then misquote it, in the gentleness and fury
of my own adult pulse, it became a new poem,
mine, it showed its influences. Even
now, I phone my sister, on this planet

calling this moon, I say "Remember?" But I can see
before, when she was just a word that touches
off a poem, when she was the knock in the marrow,
and I remember: My father dries his hands.
The moon's a hardness, on softness. He's writing a poem
in my mother, called "A Second Son," she's
writing a poem around my father
as if he were its subject. Hers, a
revision of his, called "Daughter," a final version. The
night means sparks in darkness, the day
means shadows like black silk slips around models' ankles.
The world says *bougainvillea,* the world says *cement,* the
planet an epic. The Chinaman starches
his poems, the little Jew on the corner weighs his
in a balance. Nobody buys poetry. Now you know
why. They're, all, busy writing it. Okay. Fine
with me. In blood, from cisterns, on walls,
by torchlight, with fasting for a week, to boozey whores,
of The Four Holy Levels, at once. I'm
writing. You're waking
from this, your pupil takes in light—so
makes a full white moon in the dark
your skull holds, a moon we
sigh over, and then write,
write poems under. It's morning. I
want to read you something.

second

—Knock.
(nothing)
—Knock. Kin Vander come out Mizzclahd? (read: Mrs. Clyde)
Yes of course boys one moment (then:) Vaaaaander

✳

You could play by the dam in Old Town. It had a bath-house and re-freshment stand, and the darky-boys who spooked their bug-eyes at you and knew about where the best places were to go turtling, they hung out there. Old Town had the bridge, and the Rock. And The Tap. In 1878, the year Bass brought his blooded lungs into Round Rock and heard their worth and let go, and the Post Office was constructed, and the Smith Hotel on West Bagdad Street: the Georgetown Railroad Company built a track, which crossed Brushy Creek just above the Rock, and there joined the main line of the International & Great Northern Railway Company. This was The Tap. When nobody was on duty, it was a natural.

✳

—Let's play Sam Bass Robs The Train and I'll be Bass.
(he robbed a *lot* of trains)
—You're always Bass.
—Well you kin be his men (turns:) 'n you kin be the Rangers (then:) 'n Vander kin be the kids 'n the ladies who get robbed 'n shot

✳

how they saw themselves: Bass (means: big, means: man-enough to-knock-the-bejesus-outa-you)
how he saw them: "No turn-around facilities were built into the track-age, so the locomotive was equipped with a head lamp and wooden cow-catcher both on the front of the engine and on the rear of the tender. It went forward pulling the train to Georgetown — then, backing past the train on a siding, coupled the front end of the engine to the southbound train and backed back into Round Rock." — inefficient, clumsy in bulk, loud, and irremediable in these vices: the same, no matter, coming or going

✳

—Hey Vander you playin or not

toeing along the track, one foot, then the other (calliope OOMpahpah, calliope OOMpahpah) like a

—Hey Vander you skunkbutt

tightrope, in time, like he saw in the lights in Austin (OOMpah, OOM-pahpah) meticulous

—Well then jes get out (a stone)

hey

—(another stone)

hey

By 1923 he

But this is 1911. He's seven, and walking away. The country around the bridge is terrible, and lush; it could be both at once, though it's hard to explain. The birds work like scissors. Plenty up there today, it's hot, if only he were somewhere . . . somewhere . . . Texas sky like a skillet, you wouldn't hold out your hand to it ever. He could be OOMpah far in these scragglebushes here, down by the mud creek, far from it all. What's this. What is it. —What lasts. Could something last thirty-three years. Sam Bass himself didn't. Look. OOMpah. —Preservation. Doesn't the world, the whole world, have an axis. Then doesn't a private world too /*flung to the wind let them slap the face of the sky for a challenge I'm S*/sssh what is it there, the total railroad planet is turning around now, Vander, Vander, what is it Vander

the pair of lavender ladies gloves

a Jewish ghetto in Mother Russia, bundled peddlerwares,
the Sabbath candles, a goat with a beard like a rabbi's. Because
he felt himself, inside himself, float—you can see
how this bridegroom, here, where *space* means *flowers,* lifts
and twists like a magic rope. Soutine
was "tenth in a Lithuanian ghetto . . . near Minsk," and came
to *La Ruche,* with mascot Roach, with roommate Hunger,
near the slaughterhouse, and knew his hanging carcasses
so, these are saints' portraits. No one had ever prayed before
in Meat Cathedral, but he did. Red was on its
many knees. It's almost night, now, isn't it?, Amadeo
Modigliani from Italy. Here you are, your table so long
and thin: the curbs of Paris. Coral nipple, in its
runs from pinks to brown, the spectrum of stiffened, posed corona, ah
your women. It happens at night and

✦

it's night. Again. Monet looks up. Monet born
in France, Monet who painted in France, and even
so: today, in France, in a real way
he's left home. He sees, the way we see in darkness, for the first time
how a rapid waver says
everything true. And sketches by taper, and so does a
little home for himself in red chalk
along the Seine—not the home that he was born into.
red smudge   The home that was born into him. / I

✦

think of an Eskimo woman
in labor. I read this once: the family gathers
and calls many names, very loud. Of course
the child will appear. But:
when the place is right, when the place is his name.

Joyce's place at the time was a little hotel
in the rue de l'Université. By the time Beach arrived
he was "almost unconscious with pain"—his wife,
the ice compresses for hours, how light now was
serrate. Dr. Borsch, a Yankee: "Too bad
y' got that kickup in your eye" and the nurse
at the clinic, "She grows garlic in a sponge
on the window, for seasonings." All this,
except the pain of course, is less
clear over the years. A specialist, Dr. Vogt, cut
into the eye's gray layer: pierced a hole.
Joyce lay bandaged for days—asked Beach to bring
The Lady of the Lake, "and read me a line."

                                        I did so,
from a page chosen at random. After the first line
I stopped, and
                    he recited the whole page
by heart and the next without a single mistake.

What perseveres. What's carried. / Monet

. . . well, "looked up" isn't exactly right. By the time
of his massive studio in Giverny, outside Paris,
glass in two thirds of the roof, he
was almost blind. But all his life,
he'd looked—really *looked:* in an all-night vigil, kneeled
at Camille's ribcage: even in grief, he'd watched as light
and death-pallor deepened through time: the ghoulish blue,
the waxy yellow; who in youth had sun go magma,
lava, orchid across her swimming voluptuous skin. So

no, not looked "up"—maybe "in" comes close: *I waited*
until the idea had taken flesh
                              and the arrangement
and composition of the subjects had of their own accord
          gradually
etched themselves in my brain . . .
                                   /for this brain,
made the right body / " 'Les Nympheas'

is permanently installed in the Orangerie,
at the entrance to the gardens of the Tuileries . . . great
hairy filaments of reeds . . . divinities . . . surfaces
clogged with cloud . . . water tips up all around us,
inspiring . . . brilliant . . . vocabulary of brush strokes . . .
enveloping welcome of the . . . germinating . . . whole
gallery seems afloat . . . incessant . . . a monumental scale"

. . . with real hope of success
I resolved to act

Sherwood Anderson acted. He wound up
in Beach's ". . . full of something, a step
he had taken, a decision he had made . . . how
he had suddenly abandoned his home and a
prosperous paint business, simply
walked away one morning, shaking off
forever respectability and security."
                              Now
here he was, in the sackcloth walls, with Shakespeare
on the signboard outside. And the books, of course.
And Beach. —Would she accompany him
to Stein's? and to his publishers? —He
didn't speak French. But here he was,
Sherwood Anderson, author of *Winesburg, Ohio,*
think of it, and his wife for chrissake named Tennessee
—*Tennessee!* In Paris.
                    All of them, so many
                        names, so many years . . .
                              Beach recalls their appearances,
                              Stephen Vincent Benét
                                    ("very serious-looking")
                                    Archibald MacLeish
                              Janet Flanner
                              John Dos Passos
                                    ("always on the go")
                        Anaïs Nin
                        Allen Tate
                  Thornton Wilder
            Henry Miller
      Thomas Wolfe
        Look Homeward, Angel
                  home
        You Can't Go Home Again
                        home

                              home
        the hundreds

having this in common by foot or in spirit
they all went to the Cirque

When Brassaï the night-stalking French photographer — idiosyncratic and compelled — discovered The Human Gorilla lodging in one of the cleaner performers'-hotels in Montmartre not far from the Cirque Medrano, it was already into the 1930's: "Bonjour. I'm Torgues. You must have heard of me, I'm famous . . .": but even then, in that last ramshackle light before it all folded up for good in '45, with the egg-pate acrobats balancing upside-down on carafes, and the snake-charmers, there in those strangely humdrum quarters where the spangled stayed, Brassaï knew what it used to be, the circus and the streetfair, in the flexed pectoral of its heyday:

"I did the stunts for Douglas Fairbanks in Hollywood and for Harry Piel in Germany . . . But . . . well, right now, I'm out of work . . ." His wife was shaking her pert cream boobs for the boys, at 18 francs a night (the subway back home ate up half). Then he "unpacked his voluminous costume," dressed. Brassaï: "Had I not known who was concealed beneath that skin

I would have been frightened" (Brassaï, who's stared the irontire-and-jackhandle gangs in the hard, scarred face when photographing their girls; Brassaï, in the pipes with the cesspool cleaners "overcome by suffocating odor"; *Brassaï*, and he would have been frightened) at this oversize, plaid-suited, derby-topped animal-in-us come out and alive. An album "displayed his feats in the ring, and also outside it, climbing factory chimneys, church steeples, bridges, viaducts . . . There were other photos of Torgues leaping into an automobile from a moving train, tumbling from a plane onto a locomotive, accomplishing unbelievably dangerous jumps" but

that was over. He was the man with the mask on his lap, a big dumb guy. The mask was squashed in his hand "Because his papers were not in order" So left for America "but without passport" leaping into the Hudson River, past Ellis "turned him over to the German authorities" Here now, by the gas heater "Torgues escaped from his irons, broke down the door to the brig" waiting for Loie to come home with 9 francs left over for milk. She danced in muslin wings, and carried them home in a neat square, to set discreetly in the shadow of his complicated craghumped unused body.

But Torgues, or someone like Torgues, would still have been high—exaltedly high—in the '20s. Everyone came, everyone brought his family for the innocent fun. Clowns carried on the grand tradition of Footit's and Chocolat's and Cha-U-Kao's lithe rainbow-costumed hijinks. Mock chariot races were held, the horses caparisoned like cream-decorated fudge, the women drivers more so. Everywhere: a child's eye was dazzled by gold braid, rhinestone-shimmered tutus, a strong man's spectrum-run of tattoos, fire-eater's saffron breath, the hoops and the smokes and the jugglers' aery concoctions, the small soft butterfly explosions of the whizzbang crackers. Poof! And stalls, *mais oui,* to purchase the sweets—those "stickies"—that brought this same exotic coloring onto the tongue. In Renoir's painting *Circus Girls,* we see the eternal naive grace of this child's-view: two preadolescents, "girl jugglers, who do not seem to know quite what to do with their oranges." (Hemingway saw that orange as marmalade-light on a young boy's smile.) They stand in their colors with such a vibrant purity, the circus reds and blues about them take on the special assertion of primary colors just let from the prism: young enough, even here, to be unmuddied.

And, also, the not-so-innocent fun . . . oh yes. Enough to have once called Toulouse-Lautrec away from cuntlap and absinthe; and, later, called that poet/artist/homosexual man's man/film director/novelist/bon vivant: Cocteau. —A face for everyone. The masochistic gentlemen with their damp eyes on the shining boots and snapwhips of the equestriennes—their haughty stare back, their lean bare legs and the shameless silked-over pout where the legs met, yesssss. The gentleladies with sadistic picks of imaginary confetti off their gowns: how they'd follow the measured roll of each acrobatic muscle over its bone, how their eyes were hungry for spotlit sweat, how they wanted a fall: from a great height, without a net, and naked. These are the people who came for the boxers in their flesh-pink vests and tigerskin shorts, who'd test the boxer's biceps and let two fingers linger like drummer's brushes stroking the longest possible langorous swish from the skins. Who lusted for corpse, who knew what to see in the greenish tinge that held a taut trapeze artiste where she hung by her teeth from an iron ring. Who understood the barely perceptible musk between the horse's back and the spread satin thighs of the rider: just a line, just a redolent line, of droplets . . .

The Big Top: planetarium ceiling with—suddenly!—the stars come close, the stars in their melon-nose, red-tights-over-a-haunch, fanged, glitter-tit blazing. This was astronomy: how every skin /like a moon/ has a dark side—the in-facing side. And here, everybody's secret dark face was safely given form. The ones who *lived* the world of inside-turned-out, who let their Gorilla be seen, were here—in trumpet, by wattage, with baubles aglow—on everyone's behalf, for everyone's hushed half.

So they came to the circus. To see performers like horse primadonna Ada Menken, who rode as one with the filigreed creature between her, who was rumored to have had an affair with the Empress of Austria; Mlle La La in the shine of the gas lamps; the pugilists Pons and Tom Cannon; the net-stockinged Mlle Elize. They came, in their hundred ways, they came.

And many came especially for Barbette.

I quote near-verbatim from the letters and journals of Jean Cocteau (with parenthetical assist from reportage by Janet Flanner):

The god of friendship has punished you for never being in Paris when we are. Your great loss for 1923—Barbette. Ten unforgettable minutes. A theatrical masterpiece . . . one of the most beautiful things in the theater . . . causing some people nearly to faint.

She moves in silence (and certainly on the first white carpet the Medrano has ever known).
diaphanous white skirts
a Chanel gown
fifty pounds of white ostrich plumes
In spite of the orchestra which accompanies the proceedings (*Scheherazade*), underlining her postures, her perilous exploits on the high wire, we seem to be seeing her act from a great distance, as if it were happening in the streets of a dream.
keeping me enthralled
the astonishing superciliary arch
a white bearskin covered sofa
Stravinsky, Aurie, poets, painters, and myself have seen no comparable display of artistry on the stage since Nijinsky . . . the wire and trapeze act . . . no mere acrobat . . . sublime . . . becomes a classic, mimics poetry itself . . . pleases those aroused by the supernatural beauty of sex.
a tightrope, and rings . . . ballet . . .
great . . . graceful . . . hanging by one foot . . .
or linking twin shadows
　　　　　. . . to fly . . .
(and after her fabulous *chute d'ange* fall, which against the blue background of the Medrano took on the mythical quality of a new Phaeton deserting the sky)
extraordinaire

in the magic light
he would pull off his wig and reveal himself as a slim, handsome young man

applausewildapplausewildapplause

. . . the curtain rises for the fifteenth time . . .

Angel, flower, bird.

Mackerel, bedbug, pig-on-wheels.
Or, in translation: pimp,
floozie-whore, police on a bicycle.
Even now, in a *quartier chaud*—a
"hot spot"—of Paris, 1920s, some girl fresh from whacking
a tripe-seller off is working her purse up
her buttocks, where it's safe, where it's heavier
now by the price of a whack. A dozen slang terms
for ejaculation, fifty for the prick, twenty the cunt,
just "to kiss": Brassaï counted thirty. There
was a house, a *maison d'illusions,* that specialized in
Japanese amputees . . . So many

                       stories in Paris!, some
opulent, some squalid. But Hemingway,
over a wheatcolor cheese and an oval wickerbasket of grapes,
decided: the Cirque. He was reporting now,
a few days, for the money. And Barbette was the rage.
La Nouvelle Revue Française ran a rave review,
the poet Paul Valéry said: "Hercules
transformed into a swallow." He'd sell. And
maybe there was this, too: repugnance.

                       Hemingway
never understood. —Who knew the rage and testosterone
of running the bulls at Pamplona, who brought Beach
boxing with the toughs and bleary promoters
of Menilmontant and the Stade Anastasie "where
the boxers served as waiters at the tables set
out under the trees," and tried "but it was not very good"
to teach Ezra Pound a left hook, who'd face the ton
charge of an elephant, yes *an elephant,* on rampage,
but couldn't face Stein, not after
she beckoned Alice: "love-pussy"—he
never understood.

             We all don't understand

something. And this was his, and
why not. ". . . you carried a knife
and would use it in the company of tramps
when you were a boy (Kansas City, Chicago
and the lake boats) in the days when wolves was not a
slang term for men obsessed by pursuit of women . . .
you had to be prepared to kill, know how, in order
not to be interfered with . . . I
thought that I had lived in a world as it was and
there were all kinds of people in it: I tried to
understand them, although
                        some of them I could not
like and some I still hated." He did try. Maybe
was still trying. —Here, where the lunch's cluster
of grapes is red in only the safe,
sober, blued-over hues of dull burgundy. Somewhere
else, in fermenting's extension, it's all drunken
tip, spin, upchuck, doublestare, go-yodel-at-the-stars.
But here . . . he looks closer, he's Hemingway, this is his
finesse: they're touched, the lacklustre skins of this bunch, with gray.
Each citizen grape in its little gray vest.

And he pays and walks fast to the Cirque Medrano.

So many stories. . . ! Not
all of them told. If this *did,* in its back-entrance
shadow, happen to Hemingway, well . . . but
that's not the point. *This*
did happen: "One day
                 while nude
in his hotel room, his face and arms covered with a skin
bleaching cream he used to remove the last
color of Texas, Barbette's

beauty ritual was interrupted as a reporter walked in on him."
(—Longstreet, *We All Went to Paris*)

looks up
surprise / embarrassment / anger / then
ho hum
bonjour
entrez vous s'il vous plaît
(lifts the lavender dressgloves and
with them makes a lavish gesture of
sit-if-you'd-like)
oom-pah-pah
je m'appelle vander clyde

You add on your hands and it's hangnail, bloodblister,
old broken ringfinger naked now after divorce . . . you
add with your abacus, go: gallstone, pain-in-a-tooth,
string of teenage VD scabs . . . My compatriots, my
generation, yes. Phil phones: Cheryl's left, they used
to punch themselves in the face for each other, doughy
and purpled, no matter what we thought of their dovecoo
attention at parties: it hurt, but now she's gone and my
god that hurts even more, and yes of course every
hangnail adds. Every bloodblister. Yes my friends, my
club. And here's the secret handshake: tremor. And here's
the secret mark: slipped slitwrist attempt. I bump into
Gloria: ad-exec grabs at her not uncomely
receptionist breasts till it's sundown, and then it's only
her own breath making weather along the
rim of a gin glass, all night, every
hush when the radio sighs static in between
the Rolling Stones and Joni Mitchell: adds. Every extra
chain and bolt on the back door, every rosewilt. My
great peoplehood, yes. The codeword: scream.
Or sigh. It's drugs it's disco it's college degree.
My dear born-in-my-year, we suffer
each other and for each other, if Fran's never left
Big David, still when Phil calls ("Jesus" long, dog, moan
"Cheryl's gone") Big David calls. Fran's lonely
in Gloria's voice, my comrades, my synchronized genes,
every pent ejaculation: adds. And I want to add
too, something about the taintstink garbageheap
in back of our houses: how every year the flowers around
are richer: how the days' crap works. Remember the little
happinesses?, my big-brutes-come-from-hatchlings,
my friends: the glints in the dark. Remember them?:
moon on a saved dime's edge, on an honest dole of
sexual glue, moon quick like a pianist's flick across a
smile in the night and isn't the music, if
intermittent, my lives-in-the-same-time, my friends, still
ecstasy? So it adds. Bloom unto bloom. If you *don't* have
a garbageheap in back of your house, still, anyway. I

mean . . . look: It's midnight. My friends are walking
out to the hill with the bent cypress, yes and
burying something there, I don't know, a box . . . a
box of multiplication tables. And under the moon's soothe,
walking back in again. Yes, many of my friends don't
live near a cypress, never have seen a cypress. But
all of my friends have walked to a cypress and back again
tonight. Do you see? By smudge-of-dirt-on-their-palms
I know them, by small-black-smear-o'-the-world. And
if I've brushed mine off a moment, if it's fallen to ink, this
ink, on a page, this page, my friends, my all-together, I'm
one of you, let me in, let me in.

third

Dr. Paul Walker, as director of the Gender Clinic at the University of Texas Medical Branch, is known to hundreds of transsexuals in the Southwest as "the Fixer." His mailbox is stuffed with importunate pleas ("I'm a woman trapped in a man's body"). When Dear Abby mentioned his name in a column last fall, he received more than seven hundred requests for surgery in a single week. "And the sad thing," says Walker, "is that the letters always begin the same way: 'I thought I was the only one in the world until . . .'" It is important to realize, Walker says, that transsexualism is only an exaggerated form of several other related gender-identity problems, an "extreme pole" on a spectrum that includes homosexuals, transvestites, persons with genital birth defects, persons whose genitals have been mutilated in traumatic accidents, criminal sex offenders, and exhibitionists. Patients in all of those categories are accepted at the Gender Clinic . . .

"So the first thing we do," says Walker, "is encourage them to act out their fantasy twenty-four hours a day. This includes cross-dressing, attending charm school—sometimes even *teaching* charm school—using the right restroom in public, and starting their electrolysis treatments . . . they tell us they are satisfied with themselves for the first time they can remember."

So. Texas, 1978. I don't know what the coterie that followed—sometimes that swaddled—Barbette, would think. It's fifty years later now and at Austin Country, a gay bar under an hour's drive from Round Rock, young transvestites perform in their rubber flamboyant parodies of feminine dress, and mouth like fish emphatically to recorded lady torch-singers. Flirt with the audience, "Honey, it took me an hour to tie down my thing," Big Pancakey Wink, "don't excite it back up now." "Shower me with applause, pretty people—or gooooolden shower me" Wiggle "from your fire hoses." They love it. Some there for a lark, some there in adolescent experimentation. Some, though—you can tell—for the first time feeling themselves fill up themselves completely. Completely, for the first time, Texas 1978, a boy from Houston tied in a bow as big as a car seat, singing to Judy Garland, let the papers take pictures, let the cops come see, look, me, me, me . . .

But in Paris in 1923, the true intemperate of the social climate could only mass, as clouds mass, around Barbette. And build up, as clouds build up, their charge. Barbette its lightning rod.

an extreme pole
Barbette dressed in storm Barbette dressed in flashing

He wanted everything.
The beetle's black armor,
its chitin, the passionless interlock
of beetle fornication, the hint of the blueprint
for a mammal's murmurous gut that a
beetle's bleak belly is, the jet lustre of it,
and how many angels and what kind
danced
Sabbath-long on the beetle's antenna . . .
Everything —Diderot. He
arrived in Paris. 1729. He passed the cobblers,
astrologers, grinders of glass eyes, tanners,
lemon vendors, sweetwink harlots with pox-blisters,
meatpie peddlers, Bible-baritone orators,
everything he wanted everything he was Denis
Diderot. He looked up. Sky black
beetle carapace. Sky with a cashew moon.
He wanted it. Wheel of cheddar moon, hoofparing
moon, halved geode moon, he wanted it, moon
the final nailhead hit in a spinning jenny,
moon the bubble a fish breaks
surface first with, moon a beetle's
last scavenged crumb, moon a jewel in the Holy Grail
still with His face reflected, bead of oil
moon and the sky black water, moon a
mandarin color, a butter color, moon pollen,
Diderot wanted it, all, more, ·
everything, "I learned
by showing others." And, so, the *Encylopédie*,
the first, the first really. Genius. From
"Abeille" to "Zend-Avesta." Diderot
—everything. From prison; in the workshop studying
gears; on the beach with a twig to the sphincters
of starfish; studying, studying,

Diderot—everything. Napoleon wanted
everything too, of course. He wanted countries.
Diderot wanted the bloom on the nap
in a square-inch of tapestry! Anybody
can want a country. He looked up, his glass
of bordeaux was half full; a good bordeaux; it
wasn't enough.

> *In spite of using terms like empty and void, the Eastern sages make it*
> *clear that they do not mean ordinary emptiness when they talk about*
> Brahman, Sunyato or Tao, *but, on the contrary, a Void which has an*
> *infinite creative potential . . .*

And Vander Clyde wanted nothing.
Sometimes, in bed, when Mother had left,
her shape remaining on the sheet was
so empty it hummed. The Round Rock
night was a black zero: nothing nothing,
then a small black ring he felt
he could fuck with his tongue. But that wasn't
nothing yet, and he wanted nothing. Whatever
it took to close your eyes in the way that made perfect
blackness blacker, or
past blacker. Into the color of nothing. No cow
with its pendulous teats in the pastor's field.
No cow the size of a neuron lighting
up eye-nerve to brain. No cow-breath, oystery,
weighting his skin. No breath
—so held it. Vander Clyde. Until the black
came blacker. And no skin. And so rubbed
creams by the hour. To rid it,
to nothing, nada, non, nyet, nein,
some days the bone could break under a snowflake,
one star was too much —Vander Clyde.
He wanted nothing.
He wanted nothing.

And then to start new.

*. . . Thus, the Void of the Eastern mystics can easily be compared
to the quantum field of subatomic physics. Like the quantum field, it
gives birth to an infinite variety of forms.*

Shimmied the lavender gloves on
up to the elbow, draped the feather boa.
A glass of bordeaux,
half-empty. You see? It
wasn't enough.

I speak of Diderot and Vander Clyde by way, through wide blurred trial,
of focusing on a glass decanter of bordeaux late in 1923. Light plays irre-
trievably in its center. Seraphic, polymorphous shape.
  —Please help yourself.
  —Merci. And . . . thanks.
There isn't much to report after all. They have their separate ways to go.
Hemingway, his clipped moustache a circumflex. (And so it said, in a
way, how to read him.) Barbette depilated and tweezed. Who'd go from
broad Texas swagger lightly to a girlish French moue, as if from trapeze
to trapeze. But something kept them there awhile, silent, uncomfortable
with each other, but silent none the less in the way communicants often
are. They had more than one glass of wine, each. Their fitful conversation
is unrecorded.

They watched the sun in the wine's red belly flicker. They were almost hun-
kered around like men in a cave, like men of the same tribe. / Then a clear
of the throat, or chairscrape. They did have separate ways, and they went.
I don't believe Hemingway even looked back (he says, in another context,
There is no mention of the Cirque) and he wrote about men against mon-
ster fish, against lions. Barbette combed the evening's wig. One hundred
strokes, and by showtime the curls were alive. By showtime he was a body
of flounces.

Or maybe they did trade a look, a moment only, in recognition.
The same itch on two such different fleshes.

This was Vander Clyde's way:

In 1911 Robert Hyland was Round Rock's postmaster. He's the one in the derby hat. The two-wheel mail route hacks were drawn by nags halfway between the stud farm and the glue plant, and they knew it, and tried hard to prove themselves, in the arid heat, in the clammy heat, the Round Rock sun an iron splat in the forge, all day along Mail Route 2. It was Carlson's route. He's standing on Hyland's right, in rumpled work clothes, with jug ears. He's standing like something extra in ears like parentheses. But he sufficed, listen:

> —Morning Mizzclahd
> Good morning Carlson. Scorcher today.
> —Yes'm
> You wouldn't be needing a sunbonnet?
> —No'm / Ah've mail
> (pause for the sun to rummage between them a little more)
> —Bills / And
> Yes Carlson?
> —this funny kind of a bill here / This
> Yes?
> —For Vander maam / Bill
> Yes?
> —board.

He was 14. He subscribed. On this day *Billboard* told him: one of the ***Alfaretta Sisters "The World Famous Aerial Queens"*** had passed away. The surviving Alfaretta placed an ad.

if he'd fit in the dead girl's costumes
if his feet minced air

he could they did *In time he went on to the "Whirling Sensations," a group that hung by their teeth on a revolving wheel and fluttered huge butterfly wings—a constellation whirling in space with mechanical and toothy ease.*

if he could be booked in England
if his sense of timing hovered like a hummingbird
if he could be booked in Paris
if his gowns were sheer with stars on
if the Princess Violet Murat extended an invitation
       her country home, the waiter serving ices and cognac, the self-indul-
       gent chat of theater directors, newspaper owners, women in jewels
       oh boar's-heads draped in a freezer-room's crystals, if he was witty
       with Texas effusiveness, if they tittered, if the gentleman would care
       for another cognac . . . ? / the Princess sniffing cocaine / the Marseilles
       bordello / his leather girdle
the Moulin Rouge
the Empire
the Alhambra
the Arlberg-Orient Express
if he could be booked in Rome
in Warsaw, in Barcelona, in Berlin, in Madrid, in Copenhagen
he traveled in style with twenty-eight trunks
and a maid "and a maid
to assist the maid"

New cane will creak ten minutes after it's used. Barbette had the best. And left his suite at the Hotel Moderne for tonight's performance. Cocteau: ". . . his face as precious as a brand-new box of pastels, his jaws enameled with shimmering gum, his body rubbed with pipe clay until it looks unreal . . ." (at the hotel, the cane chair Hemingway used has just now stopped complaining; the room is silent; the fixtures gleam and later after the show there will be fourteen bouquets like peacocks' lavish sexual fans) ". . . the dresser helps Barbette into his gown, fluffs the feathers, hooks up the bodice . . ."

spotlight: full, round, moon
       gray splotches: the man in the moon
on the back of a gown
       that turns
around into the Goddess Diana
       in gold and silver and lucent mesh

ahhhhh ". . . Thanks to Barbette, I know that it was not just for reasons of 'decency' that great nations, great civilizations gave women's roles to men."

The swayback chairs in Round Rock had stopped their creaking long ago. Round Rock was silent now. The whole world was silent, and watching:

if he'd swing trailing meteor-fire
if he opened like a nosegay
if he made the highwire a spine
   for a great transcendent body of Female-Being

theylovedhimtheycheered   he threw them his gloves in aloof affection, one long lavender arc (*to the wind let them slap the face of the sky for a challenge I'm S*)kin with handfuls of cold cream . . . blond wig . . . this unforgettable lie!" -Cocteau / They stood on their chairs now applauding.

every movement made perfect and in place
and a perfect place made

". . . grafting is necessary to obtain grapes whose wine has a satisfactory taste. A work recently published describes the American vines best suited for stocks and specifies the French vines that can be grafted on them to advantage."

Scientific American

March, 1878 the year of the death of Sam Bass the Wild West's greatest Outlaw buried at Round Rock Texas United States of America amen

A toast: "To ———"

Who? There was much of masking. Brassaï's mechanical eye records the costume fests of Bal Bullier where the Montparnasse artists came for their gala whoops, to choose "the most beautiful model," here where the lava-redhead woman "the Pantheress" held court. And at the Interns' Ball "everyone was naked. Some covered their bodies with glitter—a mixture of gold dust and beer," the girls "determined to spend the night on their backs with their legs in the air." At the Bal des Quat'z Arts "the theme was changed every year—Incas, Aztecs, Phoenicians, Egyptians, Gauls" but "there wasn't much fuss about historical authenticity. The men wore decorated jockstraps, the women transparent muslin. They made up for their lack of clothes with turbans, pointed hats, pagan jewelry, make-up. Everyone was covered with paint: red, bronze, gold, silver. Their faces were smeared with burnt cork." And then his photos of women (resplendently coiffed, décolleté) dancing with women (blunt sailor's cut, roué's tie-and-tails, the stub fingernails and cigarette angled hard from the lips' far corners: look of a dockworker out for his night on the town) and elsewhere, veiled, hoseried, pearled and thick-rouged: men with men. Cocteau, directing *The Blood of the Poet*, included a scene for his patroness the Victomesse des Noailles: "a small part seated in a theater box." But "when she saw the final version, the victomesse objected, finding it too broad and shocking." The scene was shot over. —Barbette in her gown and jewels.

But surely *the* grandiloquent and most mature example of masking is Cocteau's film version—literal, to its credit avoiding the campy, the satiric, and the easily surreal—of Madame Leprince de Beaumont's story for children, *The Beauty and The Beast*. Every frame is a perfect study. They pass like a celluloid freight train: each car, one further nuance of cargo from another world. Jean Marais is The Beast. His stature a king's, his raiment gilt-stitched. His face a fanged lion's. I want you to see it: the long yellow teeth, the brute fur, the mane, the misshaped ears. And the knowing human eyes. / Not everybody, I guess, is moved by Disney's ducks—though some of the comic book art in the '40s and '50s makes them, I think, exact though simplified expression of everyday wants, frustrations, and victories in the world of *homo sapiens 20th century*—simplified, and so: emblematic. At their best they're not ducks anthropomorphized, so much as they're my friends in delightful rudimentation (the artwork by Carl Barks is best). Sometimes just the upturned lilt of an orange bill . . . But few of my friends are convinced. It's Cocteau's triumph here, that even the most relentlessly sophisticated are stirred by The Beast's unexpected displays of tenderness, sorrow, and gallantry. They're stirred where they're preconscious. —Where they're sure *their* best selves too are sometimes eyes gone lost in the vast shaggy veldt of what seems to be ugly and dangerous. He breathes through a damp grainy snout. But we see, after a while, by Cocteau's signs, what—after a while—Beauty sees.

Josette Day is Beauty. Her most famous scene is: when she enters The Beast's domain down that long, that very long, dark, very dark, stone hallway. I'm not sure of the technique (a part of the movie's power: one cares enough in the characters to *not* be concerned over special effects) but she's probably in motion along a conveyor belt of sorts, dark, blended with background. And so she appears to float, slow and even, this blonde, this pale face, this white wraith's gown about her. I want you to see it: the heavy black planet, a frail blanch motion of dress. Along a conveyor belt. —As if supplying charge, generating spark, for the whole of the plot, for all the players, for life in its farthest bizarrebent extensions.

You know it: eventually she loves him. There's that flash of moment, he seems to be dying, she runs *Ma Bête! Ma Bête!* and kneels to cup his animal lips a final drink from her own pliant hands. There's glow (the film, in gray and shadow, is cornucopiac with glow), there's narrative symmetry—and then The Beast *is* Jean Marais—his cheekbones planed by lighted air itself, in clothes of most courtly splendor, handsome, close to effeminately handsome—they rise, kiss, couple, into cloud. Our first, most noble, reaction is: joy for the lovers (again, I think, a tribute to the film). And then, as the theater bulbs flush and the world our world rushes in: more self-concerned: don't we turn, though perhaps in imagination only, to The Invisible Partner who's straightman, confidante, a-shoulder-to-lean-on: and wink: and go: see, who was in me all along?

✳

Ask Torgues, The Human Gorilla. He'll tell you. But don't ask him now. He's busy feeding Peter his six-year-old flaxen-haired boy, from the last of the milk, and Peter's giggling, Peter's all pink and wobbly and giggling, the way he always gets when father puts on the mask and goes Boo!

A toast

"Security,
receptivity,
enclosure,
nurture
—these functions belong to a woman;
and they take structural expression
in every part of the village . . ."

Round Rock

*/ by night. She hangs her dress in his room, now he's gone. And it's white
a long while, even in this backcountry blackness—a pale flicker, Beauty
itself. The final lingering thought in a brain, before sleep's total blankness.*
". . . in the house
and in the oven, the byre
and the bin, the cistern,
the storage pit, the granary, and
from these pass on to the city . . ."

Paris

*/ lights itself. A million wicks, of a million kinds, but ultimately: the one
kind: everywhere, men are toasting women. Or maybe that's just a way of
saying: Barbette sips a last glass of wine before sleep. He wishes well for
himself.*
"Every construction
and every inauguration of a new building are
in some measure
equivalent to a new beginning,
a new life. And every beginning
repeats the primordial beginning,
when the universe first saw the light of day.
Even in modern societies, with
their high degree of desacralization,
the festivity and rejoicing
that accompany settling in a new house

still preserve the memory of
the festive exuberance that,
long ago, marked the *incipit vita nova*."

Still

life: a table, some chairs, a sheeted figure in bed, in sleep's placidity. Everything fits, and balances. There's been a party: a few glass-brown champagne-bottle shapes, a general happy disorder, flowers: fourteen showpiece bouquets. So: quite a party. And now it's done its work, it's dark, the shape on the bed breathes steady, out the window we can see the moon: it too, like the breath, is a rhythm, it too, like the breath, repeats. A wineglass on the table, with a single scarlet lemon-wedge of lipstick at its rim. The hands of two svelte lavender gloves are clasped: accidentally perhaps, casually to be sure—and still they're a prayer. They're a voluptuary's prayer. And if they're asking for a kind of rightness, something's efficacious here: the window breathes with the sleeper, the moon is plentiful. By its light, we're drawn to the table of dainty makeup pots, their vibrancies: tansy, Nubian kohl, bunsen blue, chartreuse, slut's red, the delicate tinge of the clam's hinge, the pearl of the clamshell's secret mantle, wimple black, a cat's-arch of comet, glint off gendarme buttons, oranges, fecal smears, a bride's ephemeral white, ink, cobalt, eggshell, fox's-tail, indigo, ember, pigeon, sourdough, strawberry, moss and veal, lime. —Monet's mixed tins of color. Having done this room in his special stroke. Having labored to do the face of this place: (fragmented, brazen, implicative, incurling, sumptuous): true to its gut.

———

This was some of Hemingway's way:

The Sun Also Rises
A Farewell to Arms
For Whom the Bell Tolls
etc.

*I took out a notebook from the pocket of the coat and a pencil and started
to write. A girl came in the cafe and sat by herself at a table near the win-
dow. She was very pretty, and her hair was black as a crow's wing and
cut sharply and diagonally across her cheek. I wished I could put her in
the story, but she had placed herself so she could watch the street and the
entry and I knew she was waiting for someone. So I went on writing. /
I've seen you, beauty, and you belong to me now, whoever you are waiting
for and if I never see you again, I thought. You belong to me and all Paris
belongs to me and I belong to this notebook and this pencil.*

Later, more specifically: the notebook
is *blue-backed*. For luck, he says, he
carried a horse chestnut and a rabbit's foot.
He gave up journalism, the hell
with the money. The stories were coming now.
And they could make do, *we had a Corsican wine
that had great authority and a
low price . . . and you could dilute it by half with water
and still receive its message.* So you could drink
at the Dome with the artists' models, and bet
sometimes on the horses, and of course the Cézannes
on the other side of the garden, at the Musée de Luxembourg,
held up their still-lives' solar, ferocious,
rinds for free. And the stories were coming.
No other thing mattered.

*Then I went back to writing and entered far into the story and was lost in
it . . . the river where I could see the trout in the pool, its surface push-*

ing and swelling smooth against the resistance of the log-driven piles of the bridge. / But sometimes when I was starting a new story and I could not get it going, I would look out over the roofs of Paris and think, "Do not worry. You have always written before and you will write now. All you have to do is write one true sentence. Write the truest sentence that you know."

. . . and I worked better than I had ever done
and rounded the park, by the rue de Vaugirard,
then home
to 74 rue Cardinal Lemoine, and into the courtyard
past the bite of the fresh-hewn lumber, and up
to the top floor where Hadley was waiting with
Bumby on one knee, who never cried, who went with Papa
to Sylvia Beach's and helped him choose the
Russian authors, F.
Puss with his large yellow eyes on her other, and
later Hemingway kissed those knees,
and more, the twigs snapped in the fire,
wife, son, all their stairs and the rabbit's foot
shiny with use for luck, not all of the rains
of Paris could wash this away, and thinking

his writing, and thinking his writing.
And thinking:

Joyce's writing:
his eyesight so battered, most found the writing illegible

Joyce's writing:
his language so ballsy, most found the writing unreadable

had gone through eleven typists
without success
when the husband of number twelve
picked up, glanced at, and
threw in the fire

France's only copy of the Circe section of Joyce's *Ulysses*

Masks false masks rubber masks masks of papier-mâché masks fastened by string by clips masks fastened by the umbilicus holiday masks and surgeons masks the masks of teenage women in blue movies masks of the children at parties masks that blanket masks that say more than the face underneath masks in plague masks glittered in mardi gras duplicitous masks masks of flesh itself masks that speak that engender that save us masks of efficacy

How Circe, sorceress
magnifique, turned men
to creatures. They rooted
swill, shat running, sniffed it, drooled.
—Homer knew. Even
blind, he'd seen
wine do such
unmasking of men, so often. I
see her: Nordic-white,
in a cloud gown. Raises,
imperiously, her hand: and Cocteau's

Beauty and The Beast, its whole train of connotation,
runs backward.

—The world being full of contrary advocates.

And now poor Circe herself
in her 20th-century role
was in peril / burnt

The full book
finally published by Beach of course
required masking
Banned
it made its way into America
as *Merry Tales for Little Folks*
"or other volumes of the right size
and with suitable jackets"

Beach: "Now it's no secret
that the hero Ulysses has friends high up,
or, rather, a friend—in fact,
the Goddess Minerva. She appears now
in one, now in another,
                    disguise. This time
it was in the very male
form of Ernest Hemingway . . ."
". . . He said, 'Give me twenty-four hours.' "

Beach rents a room in Canada
          Hemingway's old Toronto friend
hundreds of copies
          one a day / huge books
"stuffed down inside his pants"
          the ferry to New York City
"great courage and cunning"
          nonchalant grin to the Port officials
a very good friend to Literature
          "must have looked like a paternity case"

"have Hemingway to thank"

who drove the ambulance without brakes in the War
who knew the cut that sawed through the bull's ears
last bastion
(last Bass-tion)
who lifted his tender shy foot like a whisper
white in the dark

—Who, finally, rescued everything.

Beach: ". . . the Germans swept over France. My student assistant did try to get away . . . machine-gunned in the ditches . . . I had a carpenter take down the shelves. Within two hours, not a single thing was to be seen in the shop, and a house painter had painted out the name, Shakespeare and Company, on the front of 12 rue de l'Odeon. The date was 1941."

The world being full of contrary advocates.

And waited. The refugees' slat-ribbed cattle grazing the Luxembourg Gardens. And waited, and ate furtive lunch with the girl required to wear the large yellow Star of David. Sun off the pinch-tipped edges of ruin and shrapnel, as if the larger blades of this war made light, the very light, bleed. And lay flat on their bellies and then the bullets, fear-piss along the cobbles, and waited.

In her restrained way: "we saw blood on the pavements . . . these soldiers were rather dangerous . . ."

Even once the Liberation of Paris was nearly complete, "there was still a lot of shooting going on in the rue de l'Odeon, and we were getting tired of it . . ."

"a deep voice calling: 'Sylvia!' And everybody in the street took up the cry 'Sylvia!' "

"He was in battle dress, grimy and bloody. A machine gun clanked on the floor. He wanted to know if there was anything he could do for us."

—Who had said *Give me twenty-four hours.* / . . . now through the room. A sniper only needs one window. And suddenly every building in Paris: window window window! Sometimes Hemingway crawled. Far off, a voluble crowd of the liberated was singing the *Marseilles*. But here the bullets were louder, and some windows showed distinct strands of smoke, as if the sky were unraveling. Out one window his friends from the other jeeps were mud streaks covering ground, then gone to other buildings. And mud streets. He thought of the color of tanks, of dead khaki, of sea when it's abused. And then like gulls or uprushed foam: a few FFI nurses over the world of dirty water: white gowns, white flags with red crosses, and white litters holding their awful poundage. On the corner a dead boy, not over seventeen, stared at the world from a neat third eye. A pistol holds six magenta flowers. Two pings, and Hemingway crawled again . . .

the whistle of a shell
the sickening whistle of a shell
and men folding
like lengths of cloth
with terrible dark dark designs on
And stood.
          -in the calm freed street-
And stood.
—sweated, harsh, eyes red-webbed and in glory
He was, after all, *Hemingway*

and his men came down again and rode off in their jeeps—"to liberate," *next, according to him, "the cellar at the Ritz."* / ovation

Though by then it was really all gone anyway. Oh, the war was won, sure. But it never should have been, this Second, the streets now deader than moon, and the Hotel Corneille where Joyce had stayed as a student: "in flames . . . destroyed." *Who's Who in Twentieth Century Literature:* "One admires Hemingway's early search" (but) "he wrote nothing of any great value after about 1940." Joyce died 1941 on the operating table. Torgues wrote Brassaï from Brighton Prison. Sherwood Anderson, '41. Scott Fitzgerald, '40. Even the songs were different. How and where the Depression left its teethmarks. Having fallen into scar when a burgundy curtain fluttered wrong at the Moulin Rouge, having felt the bones turn, back in America in 1938 in a vaudeville grind house, Barbette caught chill backstage and developed pneumonia / "surgery" / "a limp in his walk" / "assisted by a cane."

it's dark oh it's dark say your prayers

Where the snake will slough its skin
/In that place let me begin
    He returned to and aged in Austin,

Where the deer will drop its horn
/In that place let me be born
    Texas. He was "the old guy with the forlorn

Where the man will change his face
/Let me waken in that place
    look"—and sometimes a brief look of solace.

✳

ah, in 1923 he . . .

✳

an iron-wire clothesline in a yard
oh listen (the drum from the circus) oom
pah and I can do that one and that one and

✳

A man looks up, in Austin, in middle July. It's the time when cicadas are bursting new and resilient from last year's pinching carapace, and the paths through yards are littered with these dry husks. From this he's learned: there will be wings—it just has to hurt, first. He's been writing a poem, so many people in it, even himself. He's been his own mask, or one of them. He's tried. Now if he closes his eyes in the blistering sun (this is true: his skin is risen and pustuled in spots, with Texas blaze) he feels the chill draft at Loew's State in 1938. The girly-girlies are chattering, pinching their tits from their pasties; then they dress, and go home, they're mothers of twins, they're economics majors. Now there's a permanent chill in the bones, metallic, something blue like a surgical pin. This could be sad. In a sad house it would be. Now this man opens his eyes. He doesn't know about his house yet, his one-bedroom apartment really. He knows about Barbette's though, or he believes he knows, though at times he believes different things. It's been a long poem, and many people have spoken in it, and many about Barbette, but Barbette hasn't spoken. The man writes. Barbette looks up (he looks up, now) on a hacienda-styled street in the deep of the Texas dogsummer.

"I felt I had found it, my city, my Paris."

Tonight, what will come of it? Earth
slips the moon like a diaphragm into the sky

/and I take down the album. Somewhere, a cop
lords it over a bum like a lumberjack
proud of his felling, somewhere a woman's taking
it all off for twenty bucks and exhibiting where
she's hinged like a mussel, and soft like a mussel,

and I take down the album,

men are discussing power
so long, their throats become doric columns, somewhere

a husband turns in a wife like a bullet
loaded then revolved, she's oiled, he
shoots the future dead. And I open the album.
And I look at myself.

Because the face is so small, from Kodak,
because the face is so small, from being five, I

hover like sun, above sun's own
intensity: white dot under a lens. And

in fact, he looks up
squinting. He must not see clearly through this

flawed twenty-five years. And somewhere a
man's pitted cheeks read like losing dice,
a flower's anthers lift their little
popesign of blessing over the field's bowed heads, do we
ever know if a cat's wail signifies love's full weight
or pain's raised hackles? Those
small pink creases x its anus
like algebraic unknown . . . The boy's

trying, he's been bent
to tie a shoe or fold an airplane
right. I see now the squint must mean effort. And
optimism. Twelve inches of night
between us—think of a black foot of earth

marked off in centuries by geologists,
how schist glints. Because

of the distance of twenty-five years, I
look at him, I feel like his father
—want to rock and hush.
Somewhere the rose, somewhere the taste of metal . . .
He's been
busy learning scar and resilient nipple, busy
making me. He's been bent to *putting-together*.
Through twenty-five years, his five-year-old's face
looks up. He says he is my father.

✻ ✻ ✻

I look up. It's true about
the night sky and the retina:
twins. The lines between the stars
are stories, Hemingway
looks up. His wife's soft
inwardpull, the poplars' allotment
of shadow—but he's writing now, he
only has eyes for my friends. Whose
names he'll never know but they're
alive on his paper, wherever human
light and salt are done correctly:
my friends are alive. Stein
looks up; some of Alice has
dried to her chin. Then writes "Now
for some if not for all

these reasons, Paris was where the
twentieth century was." Then tends
the fire. Upturned zombie's eye,
the moon. The moon a lactal
bead of the heavens. Baby's-belch moon,
moon rifle sighting,
                    today I saw a bird
on a wire. So thought of Barbette. A
speculum moon. Moon firemen's net.
Blind brass coin on a black mantilla.
Heroin-sparkle on dark pomade,
                              moon,
let me lay down in a saline solution.
Let me be. Let me just rub my face
in bermuda grass and sleep. Let me beat
in a cave with the fatted bears,
slow. Moon, embalm me; just
eight hours or so. Moon, faience
pendant on Tut's chest, mummy me
just for the night. Let me stop.
Let me run out of ribbon. Pay the sitter,
go home.
         The jism
crackles, my sister Livia's born. And
now here she is with a white bouquet like a
great fresh handful of nerve-end,
marrying. Joyce looks up—he's getting it
down, tonight while no one can sleep and
Brassaï fits a plum-bosom body
from the Follies into his own black
night in the night, a word at a time Joyce
knows it, says it. Knucklebone
moon and moon a sweet
swiss cheese, the moon
cross-section of hardon, the moon a
nun's mouth: o of praise,
moon punctuation ending it all.
Let my friends Jim and Jean buy an Oregon farm,

and milk, and pomegranate. Let
my friend Tony Sobin say a name inside the gray ear
of the mare, which is shape-of-a-mosque,
and go home, and she's there. My parents
lay down by each other: an
equals-sign.
                    Moon
witch's last tooth awobble in the deep.
Moon ball of air in a hypodermic.
Moon zero, moon amoeba, moon blastospore,
shut up. You're too serious. Give me
my half of the blanket, moon, and let's
call it a day. Let me sing.
It's a lullabye: *Fill In the Blank,*
you'll like it. Let me fall
plunk with the lemmings through the first
small gap in a dotted line. And
dream there. I was a fish once. Even
now I like to lick women where they come
closest to gill. Let me dream it,
rough with blood. Moon honey
Moses promised the Children of Israel,
moon a jewel in the Sacred Arc
they bore across sand, let me be
with my head full of nutsy-stuff, maybe
I'll see holy folderol lightning like life
across Frankenstein's bolts, only
give me the chance, go away. Let me snore
through my blubbery supper.
Moon blurred face of the anaesthesiologist.
Let the cat out, roll over.
                    Fitzgerald
looks up; and coughs like a miner. And like a
miner, carries a canary
into his lowest work. He'll die of the lung but the
song will be in it. And so I
think of Barbette. The moon a dime, the night
a phone-gut. Rings—my sister

looks up. We talk, somewhere
a bird on a wire, a bird for a sign on our talk.
Let the squid be ink, the goose
be quill. Let poets in Paris write.
Let my friend Wayne Zade in Missouri write.
Let Ezra Pound write from the booby hatch,

                                    moon
tug the dangerous waters, moon give
fish wings. Moon monthflood, one red wing
on each of Micheline's thighs, and
Carolyn's thighs, and somewhere Ellen's.
Moon bubo, moon dot
of light on a heron's black jelly eye,
moon leucocyte: heal. Oleo,
spermbubble, droplet of Lourdes,
moon: make whole. Yeast moon
rising. White
pottery sherd. Moon marble
veined blue, moon dove's egg, moon
lint on a governor's tongue, moon
cyst, moon crystal of sugar,
shine.
        For my friend Mimi Bardagjy:
show us a map of the palm. For Diane
amok in New York: of the hooks in the cortex. In Syracuse,
Robert Lietz, with Arlene Lietz now three weeks
in her beautiful stewy diapers: of every vein
of suck in a mother's breast, to a daughter's first
lips' pursing. Shine,
you hear? Make it gentle. Circles of sweat
on a trumpeter's lip, and gaslamp-yellow
makes of it: full, half, quarter, slivery
lunar calendar. On a black lip, yeah good jazz,
and my friends look up. A woman's
on a wire. In a man.
                Oh
swami, rabbi, priestess
moon. Moon wafer of

transubstantiation, moon
hole-for-the-fuck-finger, moon
altar, moon polar cap, moon cyanide pill.
Moon drop of maplesap,
moon drop of snakevenom, moon
celestial nut-and-bolt where the
caliper's arms attach,

                        let me measure you,
let me make a shape, moon clay,
moon swell-o'-the-belly.
Let me wake, just a minute,
easy. And wash. And
build something, just something
little: an hour. Let me breathe into it,
like a balloon, okay? See it,
there? on the clock? this
round-thing, this start, this
morning moon. This bird,
this wing of the bird, this quill of the wing,
this barb of the quill. Blurred face
of the midwife, hovering, moon this
barbette. An anointing
with creams. Backstage, every night;
a reporter saw it. Self-christening. Hello,
Myself the Champagne Bottle over
Myself the Ship's Impeccable Bosom. Then won't
the fragments fly! Monet will do it. Let him
study the colors of Vander's lotions. In Paris,
remember Paris? Then everyone
sleeps. I mean everyone, like 'em or not.

                                     I
look up. It happened this way. And
some of them slept with Clock-in-the-ribs,
or Brick, or Billfold, or Plasticine.
—But I mean *my* friends, vulnerable and raw.

Everybody with a heart was looking for a skin.

Notes / Acknowledgments

Person-names, place names, dates are true. Most (not all) material in quotes and italics is true to some source—though spliced for my purposes. Everything not true to verifiable fact I've hoped is true anyway to a verifiable spirit—keeping in mind Lily Tomlin's character Edith Ann: ". . . and truth can be made up, if you know how."

For Barbette: Longstreet's *We All Went to Paris,* the journals of Cocteau, a moment from Janet Flanner. For the writers' lives: those obvious invaluable sources, Beach's *Shakespeare and Company,* Hemingway's *A Moveable Feast.* For Texas: Martin's *Sam Bass the Bandit,* The Round Rock Kiwanis Club's *Round Rock, Texas, U.S.A.!!!,* and *The Texas Monthly* (John Bloom) on "juggling sex in Galveston." For Brassaï: his own compelling *The Secret Paris of the 30's;* for a bit on the Parisian Cirque: *Montmartre* by Philippe Jullian. For Eastern sages, Woman's expression in architecture, and the inauguration of a new building: from "Thoughts on Sacred Space" in an issue of *Parabola,* quoting (in order) Fritjob Capra, Lewis Mumford, Mircea Eliade. And, for Monet: Y. Taillendier's *Monet* and quotes on "Les Nympheas" from Sarah Newmeyer and Michel Butor. Other, momentary, sources are credited in-text.

applausewild is inspired by Arthur Vogelsang.

THE
CENTRAL
LIGHT

a selection of poems

1981–1993

Wings

I always wondered why they called them wings.
—Perhaps because somebody always waited in shadow
in them, with a rope.
With a rope like a great braided nerve,
and while some sweet singing or bloody melee
completely filled the central light, this person
would raise or lower the god.

It's summer. Hard summer; the land enameled.
I find the bird already half-dismantled
by ants—the front half. It's flying
steadily into the other world, so needs to be this still.
Do I mumble? yes. Do I actually pray? yes.
Yes, but not for the bird. When we love enough
people a bird is a rehearsal.

"Bird

Satificate." That was what my grandfather's English heard, and how he labeled it. The creases, a century old, are sharp, as sharp as a whiff of ammonia, and they seem to be the replicating image that gives character to the bank where the document's stored: the hard geometry of what money means in America. Teller's smiles you could cut a week-old crust of cheddar with.

Its duplicate information might still be in Germany, in village records stacked in a cellar, beneath its one bulb's drone. A century past, the clerk fastidiously nibbed the information in, the squat black script as heavy as a branch. And a flourish, maybe you could almost say a flower, that was my grandfather's name. Perhaps the clerk didn't need a new gold tooth after all, or the rashes on the cow's teats went away overnight, who knows? But by that final cursive gaiety, we understand him. Then he went on: somebody's geese for the tax-count, somebody's *zaydee* dead and the coffin cost so much in terms of tins of tallow, somebody's fresh wet field of rye.

And then he'd immediately forget. And then the owner of the geese or the rye immediately forgot. It's what writing's for. It changes the content of an oral tradition's storage system. The brain can afford to give off the aroma of facts in mulch, the glow of facts in foxfire, yes the click of facts in carbon dating. —Somewhere, in documentation, it exists: eternal present tense. Sixteen geese and a rye crop.

I think everyone's known the sensation. You wake—it's dark, and the night and your skin don't show exact delineation. The air is rubbing like a cat at your ear, for admission. Last night I woke—I'd dreamt that I was a limb chopped off a greater body, which still tried to move me and wept. I almost heard the weeping. It was happening in a corner, and there were other sounds, not all unhappy: a fiddle, an animal snort, the thin cool slide of a picture's hanging-wire being positioned carefully on its nail. There was a record kept in the air, in atoms, perhaps in between the atoms, a permanence. I was only a man with his hearing accidentally against that lock's invisible tumblers' turn.

In the spring, a swallow always returns—across the thousand aerial miles, fright and flux, to its own one place. *This* swallow, year after year, to its half-moon hole in the eaves of the court building. See it? —wobbly a moment. This is the year the village is gone. A German village, of tinker Jews, and it's been razed—by fist and by fire. So much char. You wouldn't think the lives of a people had this much ash to start with. Now it's stopped its wobble, it's hovering like a hummingbird mid-air. Above where the records-books once were. So calm, so effortless—there isn't a branch but it looks as if it's perched on a branch.

Gallery

When my grandfather stepped from the boat
they gave him a choice of paintings to enter. "This one,"
he said by a nod of his head. Why not?—for weeks
in the bodystink quarters of steerage,
the lice had run as freely as milk through his crevices,
and the only food was saltbread softened in engine water,
but here, in *The Boating Party* by Renoir, it's spring,
the light is floral, even cloth and skin
are really petals in this light, the glass
the wine is in is alive in this light, the men are easy
in speaking with women (he noticed, oh especially,
the women), their mutual fascination is another flower
filling the air, and the clusters of fruits
looked as shining to him as an orchestra's brass section
—when he peeked around the corner of the painting, in fact,
he saw a grouse was simmering in peppered cream
and that settled it, he sat down at a nearby table,
listening to the bright and empty talk, his shy eyes
staring at his waiting plate. A server appeared
and left. On my grandfather's plate was a boiled potato,
only that. But he was starving, so he ate it. He ate it
indelicately, with an almost sexual fervor, and then
looked up to see the family around him,
with their corded hands, with their faces like worn-out shoes,
were eating theirs, just that, with a root tea. He
was in Van Gogh's *The Potato Eaters*. The room
was as dark as the tea. Outside, the wind was a punishing switch.
The talk was hushed and raw and familiar,
he was at home here, he was at home in the broken
light of the hanging oil lamp. When the meal was done,
he stepped out into the lane, he breathed the country dark in
hungrily, then walked. He needed a wife.
He needed a future. What did he see ahead,
when he squinted? He would barely understand

that man in Edward Hopper's *Nighthawks,*
on a distant corner, some depleted 3 A.M.,
was his son—who slides the dime for his java
over the counter, slants his hat, then heads out into streetlight
from the diner's unrelenting angles and planes.
He's lonely. It's 1942. He'd love to meet my mother,
someone humming a hot little tune
and pretty as a picture.

First Ride & First Walk

Finally my heart stopped murmuring.
They lifted me from the glass case
in my week-old sleek pink skin.
Daddy Irv was shnookered already
on good news and better *schnapps*. They
say he fixed me in the carriage's
boy-blue swaddle and then took the snakey
paths in Humboldt Park with his
left hand a bountiful humidor, his right
on the handle supplying whoopsie
steering, and my name angled bright in
his breath like a swizzle stick. Mommy
found him, hours later, by then the
cigars invisible but offered with equal
panache. I was gooing. He was singing
Hey Theodora, Don't spit on the floor-a,
Use the cuspidor-a, That's what it's for-a.
Grandpa Louie led him home. A diminishing
trail of for-a's through the dark. I
never pleased anyone that much again.
The park was safe in those days; Mommy
Fannie just stood there, watching me cry,
then lifted my plum face soft to her nipple.
What a day. I dozed, then. And she
left the carriage there—it could wait
for tomorrow, those days were full of time—
surrounded by grasses and me at her breast.
Walking home in the deep green silence, a cow trying
hard not to ring its bell.

Steerage

*. . . inferior below-decks accommodations on a ship: by
extension, the whole of a certain kind of immigration as the
poor experienced it*

By now, the satchel's leather has reclaimed its living redolence,
it riles at the hasp, and reaching inside it is entering
up past the wrist in the vault of an animal body. Here

they are, in the various tea and fecal colors
of early photography: my grandparents, carrying everything
Europe crammed in a single bag. This

bag. Clumsily held on his shoulder, like a hod, perhaps
to ease an earlier posture. Waiting. One of the first of the lines,
I think—the oily air of the ship's pit still on their faces: it

may be the only thing reproduced here in the original hue.
So now this satchel has its miniature replica floating inside
its belly: a strange idea, vaguely canopic,

soul-like, or homuncular—eldritch, at least. They're
eldritch too, on the dock in their Cracow woolens: little
people, 3, 4 inches, yes, look: I can hold them in my palm

like in the stories. The wee folk. The thumblings. Everywhere,
these old ones, the root ones, have their stories, and
gain strength as the dusk along the woods duff deepens:

menehunes, filing through gates of Hawaiian guava, mango,
for a moment their eyes like budding fruit
the moon lights in the lavish branches; brownies,

kaukases, domovniks, pukys (our Puck) . . . the global
elvish, faces fresh as a thimble-diameter of cream
or puckered like overbathed toes. The nisse, the deive,

the forthright English sprite . . . with their credos,
their language, and their acorn-color aprons or radiant
cobweb negligees . . . every night, through the portals, from their

great ancientdom, into the settlements we've made
the planet's governing order. Darkness
is their steerage; and in it they enter that order,

comprehending or not, however best they can. We
all do. I remember (I was maybe 5, I barely came up
to the bathroom doorknob) tumult over my father's

failed attempts at happily sorting family business
in the files of City Hall. Some long, grandparently
problem, I guess now: rights to property, or citizenship,

who knows? I watched the man who fed me,
flung me, beat the neighbor hound away, walk
dwindling into a building the size of an ocean liner and

walk out hours later looking simply used up. Because
we're little—people born into a giant's land
of bureaucratic backrooms and, beyond it, the universe

stacking matter and antimatter—we have these secret
handshakes, satchels of family heirlooms, private songs . . .
whatever it takes to personalize and console. He

was shaving. I stood by the bathroom door and watched
him suds the mug, then tauten the grain of his neck.
He didn't know I was there. He whistled,

that tune *his* father whistled. Maybe it made the whole damn
day wash away. I think I could whistle it too, a goofy
old world melody—by which we mean there are some of us who

have heard a music that's not of this world.

Semiotics / The Doctor's Doll

Traditionally, a Chinese physician respected his patient's modesty by offering her a small doll, sometimes ivory and beautifully carved, of the female anatomy. She would receive this through curtains, mark her complaints on appropriate parts, then return the figure, "examination" completed.

—SOSHO

I.

A small rock braids white water
in blue water. This is why
I think of the stream as a woman
lying face down—that lazy

pigtail, and the little curve
of a waist later on. There even may be
a woman, or man, real, flesh,
nearby for whom this stream is

a summarization—as the desert's red
dementia-spill at sunset, and powder
to cobalt blues of its clearest
daytime heights, became

the shingle in front of O'Keeffe's shack.
There are signs, they say
a thing when a thing is lost
to other saying. This explains

art, and why a peach by O'Keeffe is eloquent
geometry of a kind
beyond a canvas's usual
linear methodology—the inexpressible

ganglia-hurts, star-stitchery and shadow-joys
of a life may find their only shameless
expression in its alive and dying
speckled sexual skin. Or

perhaps it's a mandarin orange
held like a crystal ball, eye-level, that
means the Emperor's favorite concubine's
future—in a garden of tended

waterfalls and peacocks, she's intent
on every ruddy pore, on each sweet meaty wedge
and on the delicate web inside the rind
like a silk map of the nervous system . . .

She's ill. It hurts, here,
and here. For reasons of her own we'll never know,
she considers the orange. For her it's a prophecy
or an insignia or a name. Or after

35 years of sharing the plumbing of heart
and backed-up bathroom, of
the diapersmear and the dollardream and the
intimate spittles of lovemaking, yes my mother's a sign

of my father. When I read her now, her face
the latest turn in a path over
six decades long, I see his face
and its gray lips smiling foolishly

in the hospital room—as if he could keep it
a secret, as if pain were not a red pet
leaping into his eyes, to look out. We'll
visit—kiss him, bring a *Playboy,* kid

about the svelte healthy beauties in there.
And later, alone in my livingroom, I'll stare
without sexuality at the vibrant vaginal lips
of a poster: O'Keeffe's *Grey Line*

with Black, Blue, and Yellow in
which two hazy body-shapes define a blue flame
that's a blue petal that's a blue
woman's rich blue sex. So I think of a stream

as a long blue human—yes, with a
scrap of ivory flotsam lodged in a bend, some
doll of what's wrong. Tonight's
symbology says a stream's a person,

so a person's in a bed. My father
weeps and weeps till dawn, in the hospital linens.

2.

Personal names, speculates Jaynes, first appeared between 10,000 B.C. and 8,000 B.C., allowing people to think about a companion long after that person was dead.

—*Science Digest*

Say these nailparings in a matchbox are somebody's
perfect reduction—and under
an incense cone, in sweat, by amber and wavery liquorlight,
a perfect badge of that person's life
is forming out of smoke to fill the room. Do
you believe it? A hundred thousand people believe it.
Say a ring of hair. Say the shaman's soul caught
in a Polaroid, it's ludicrous but
then why is he gasping for air on the mat, for days now?
Everybody's read some version of that story
in which the dollhouse burns, and half a country away
so does the fullsize house it's modeled on. We all
have a doll of ourselves—a child, a wife,
a protegée, taking our tightrope walks and faith healings
into a foreign land. We've all repeated the simplest lesson
of algebra up at the blackboard, teacher
pointing with much-frayed patience at the *x*, while
we say: *stands-for.* Say it: stands for.
                          Say
the Master's gospel in proselytizers' ardent
renditions, say the bloodstuffed tampon, say
your own self caught in a Polaroid
25 years ago there like a two-inch doll
at the algebra blackboard, say the sign of a person,
say a name.
             —An old name, Albert, my
grandfather's name and then mine. So now I'm his
ambassador, from a world
of ghetto donkeycarts, fat Sabbath candles, soupsteam
fogging the windows, and a voice in blessing hovering
like God's own special hummingbird over the wine . . .
—Or older, a clan-name, a cave-name,

Runs-With-The-Bears, Old-Trout-Mouth,
a beast-name, a bird-name . . .
                              Say she's
Fei Yen, *Flying Swallow*. She undoes
her nighttime pigtail slowly, as if divvying
gold spoils after a battle. And there's been a battle,
in her system, all night. She hears the doctor's pony
stamp where it's tied to the plum in the yard,
she can imagine its breath in the cool dawn light as heavy
as a feedbag at its muzzle. Her bed is as blue as a stream,
and her azure robe, and the blue brocade that blocks her
from the sight of any male save the Emperor and
his eunuch. Even her slippers are blue, on the blue shelf.
No wonder she looks at the orange. It
jumps like a flame in her tired eyes. And then the hangings
part, and in a pair of polished rosewood tongs
is the doctor's doll. She holds it as a stream
might hold the map of a stream. She runs it
down her body.
                    Once I saw one—an exhibit
at the Denver Art Museum: one entire body done
from one sleek muscle of ivory. She was maybe
a foot long, lustrous and lush, reclining
frankly on a small dark wooden couch—the pale
swell of her nudity framed by a deep blue tortoise comb
in her hair, and sharp black lacquer shoes—civilizing
endpoints. She smiled. Her thighs were coyly crossed.
They made the x I must have thought of all the while
my algebra teacher tried to conjure some right answer
out of my adolescence. She told me x was a sign
for the great unknown. Man, was it
ever! Then sat back on the edge of her desk
where her lean white hosieried knees were the dials
that tuned in all of my daydreams, she was angry
with the things I didn't know, and
so was I, in my own way.
                              Signs,
and more signs, and how to read them. Flashes

like quick carnations of light
in 19th century telescopes—could these be
signs of life on Mars? Could these be the blasts
of canal construction? Signs: the *feng,*
that fantastical bird with the head of a pheasant,
the neck of a swallow, a dragon's wings and a peacock's
ostentatiously plumaged rump: whose appearance
presages virtuous rulers, therefore whose depiction is the
aegis of auspicious reign (one's done in gold and turquoise silk
on her bedcurtains by the Emperor's decree: a *hwang,* a female
feng: "In poetry, many allusions to sexual pairing
are made by reference to the fidelity of *feng* and *hwang.*").
Signs: my grandfather's *yarmulke,* also
silk and also blue—it was the likeness
of the sky his God presided over, and made the most delicate
touch of that glory on his head, for his whole life,
as long as his life was. Now it's mine. And now
I'm his, as the track of a man belongs to that man,
if a track can be left ahead, in ground
a man will never touch, if a track can continue without him.
Often I walk the night and wonder how
many emblems and deputies we make of ourselves, or even
have the empathy to see
in the makings of others. Signs: she was,
as I remember it now, a substitute teacher.
X, she said, on somebody else's behalf. Some nights
I see that mark, in the air, meaning here,
and here.
                    She lets the doll back out
through the curtains. Inkbrushed dots say pain
along its naked length, and say it in hope
of pain's negation. Then she sleeps. Sleep feels as if
a giant doctor's hand is holding her, then placing her
in a deep dark pocket. The pony starts its journey . . .
Say she's my father's name.
Then say my father's name.

3.

In Jewish tradition to this day the name of a person who is critically
ill is sometimes changed in order to confuse the Angel of Death.
— NOAH JONATHON JACOBS

those clouds in the north
heaving with everything
planet and sky cycle through them
there is a pain in my lungs

this is the leech I have taught
to squeeze itself out
of itself as a symbol
can you help my heart

they give you a number and
then a gown and then a little gauzy mask
I saw him once a cipher
between the check-in and the check-out desk

this is a man on a bed like an entry
written in the book of names
he is Frank he is Red he is Jennifer
he is registered as James

there is no Irving Goldbarth here
there is no Irving Goldbarth here
the needle will wink and the blood will follow
this is the bed of Flying Swallow

this is a prayer I say to the angels
low on insomnia high on dope
dozens of yesterday's specimen vials
are saying a man to the microscope

this is the bed of Flying Swallow
this is the truth now disappear
this is the bed of Flying Swallow
there is no Irving Goldbarth here

Coin

When the surgeons slit into my father they went to Jupiter
they went so far, to a barren red moon of Jupiter's.
I'd never been there. My mother had never been there
in him, to a cave on that moon, to the runaway vein
that snaked some inner wall. And even this they slit
and entered, with their geiger counters that fit in a pore.
They needed to hear its half-life keening wildly. There's
one red anti-meson in everyone—here, at this, even
they stopped. Here, at this, my father turned them back,
as all of us were turned back, and he stayed
—as everybody stays, no matter the opening up—
alone in his pain. The microlasers won't usher you there;
or love. In everybody, there's this final landscape
only capable of supporting a population of one.
I was thinking of this as the bus pulled up,
the last bus of the night, at the hospital stop.
It must have been the amber window squares of buslight
in the 3 A.M. pit-dark—I saw that painting of the 18th century
doctorpharmacist Michael Shuppach, studying
a beaker of a patient's urine, meditating, empathizing,
making the late Swiss afternoon light do great
disclosing swirls around that honey and its sediment,
more intimate in ways with this woman than any
deep sexual splitting-apart or any kneeled confessional
admission . . . down to the single citron valence-of-her,
in its nakedness, in his crystal. There's
one golden anti-meson in a life; and here, even he stopped.
There was only one passenger riding the bus: one face
staring out of a window. Someone
needing a bus at 3 A.M. with a story of why
—for a second, before I stood to board and then
decided not to board, our eyes met,
starting a common exchange. —Then
the face shut like a change purse, over
its single coin minted on Jupiter.

Again

There was such darkness in him then. And I repeated,
at the bedside, something—what, I don't remember exactly but
something simple, something with the desperate hope we find
inside ourselves at times like that, it might have been only
don't let him die incanted until it transcended being
words, or even prayer, but was a relegation of breath to that preliterate
place faith comes from—something meant to be a chain or list
of small lights through his darkness. So I thought of Japan,

the *Sheet of 1,000 Buddhas:* how a single woodblock stamp has meant
so many duplications of the same small holy figure—each,
its nimbus; each, its dole of glow to keep back its commensurate
dole of benightedness. They finally make a pattern each is
lost in: each a quantum of light, in light. In fact in A.D. 770,
the Empress Koken commanded one *million* prints of a Buddhist charm
be stamped by copper blocks, "to ward off illness" says the story,
    which is
this story as well. And if I digress right now to the story

of Chunosuke Matsuyama who, in 1784, wrecked half-dead on a coral
    reef
with 43 others, scratched his story of woe and goodbye on wood and
slipped it with ritual into a bottle, then the bottle in the swift Pacific
    drift . . .
it doesn't mean I've forgotten that hospital bed, my father
dwindling in it, or the mission of this poem. But
there's a bottle, under sun and over sunfish, blue in cerulean waters,
jet in black, and later I'll return to it. Repetition is what
this poem is about, repetition is what this poem is about.

Even in the oldest stories, it's always 3 wishes, always
3 importunate *open sesames* at the lamp cache's sandstone door.
Luck thrives on serial attempt: perhaps because luck knows how
failure comes first. The ploughboy in the Japanese fairy tale
needs succeeding at 3 tasks (make fire from water,
etc.) before he's awarded the princess's hand. But oh,
time is longer than fortune, my dearests, my sweet ones.
Read the wedding banns 3 times and thrice fling rice, yet

I've seen Jimbo's marriage undo one dawn like a sparrow
their tom brought, head half-hinged and brains sopping out, with
delicacy to their doorstep. Nothing assures. One night
I opened the door on my wife in a terrible, naked parallelogram
of streetlight on the bedsheets—nearly crushed by the light,
so weak she was then, and crying into her hands and God's ear
why me why me why me: and I understood that 3-time cry
reversed us back to zero. Even so, we try; in the face

of everything shaking its great head *no,* we try
to hold on to whatever little over-and-over-again shapes
methodology from nothing . . . The nightshift nurse. I'd
watch her smooth the bed or sometimes his forehead
past smoothness, and into a level of ceremony
purely. —20 shakes of the thermometer. And 19 of them
unnecessary—unless needing wishing is necessary. Just
one rub at the genie's lantern never efficacious.

Of course I visited. And my sister. My mother
kept absolute vigil. And even so, I know he was alone
inside the tubes. I know I'd stand there trying to think myself
immeasurably into the cells, the sick ones, down the fundament of what
we are, to where it all begins, and by such empathetic thinking
burnish the blastula of him clean . . . But no, the tubes, the tubes
are insular. Pain is insular. And the glaze across an eye.
Even my ex-wife offered to phone him—Morgan. Her name is

Morgan. My father's, Irving. I say this in attempt to bring you
closer by that nominal bit—you, whoever you are "out there,"
Venusian in your distance from these people I love—you, reader.
If I told you that the night nurse is Arlene? Arlene
Bedoya. And I never did find out the name of her "strange
husband" "in Miami" "wit that batch" although I later learned
the batch's name was Topsy, so heard it correctly:
estranged. She hopes "to win me back his ol heart." I know

at shift's end, in the weak leaking out of Chicago's first
dirty light from the skin of the lake, she goes home and
runs her hands over the Christmas gifts she's wrapped for him
—it's only October—over and again, as if to build up some
electrical charge that might power her love clear to Florida. I know
I made of myself a present to my father in that same way, wanting
some volt to accrue that would heal—so, yes, I visited him,
I watched for a spark, I visited him repeatedly.

✦ ✦ ✦

The last of his tasks. All dawn the sky more milky-gray
than a fish-innard condom. Now, though, sun
breaks through; and on a high plateau of comb-grass where the dew is
still a sticky kiss on everything, he picks one bead of it
up in a knotted stem and, with the patience of the poor-for-generations,
focuses sun through. Fire. From water. Winning the princess's
hand, and the princess's sweet cream-bodied breasts, and . . .
enough. Let them couple alone in a cloak of the Japanese night,

in love the whole length of their story. And Tony
and Sharon; and Karen and Danny-in-Drag; and the Wolkens . . .
in love their whole length. And then? And then, and then.
When Jimbo knocked at 4 A.M. his gut was on his tongue.
"We split up." *snap* "Like that." All over, entire cities, 4 A.M.,
the tiny bones of whole lengths breaking *snap, snap, snap* . . .
Now what to tell our Nipponese sweeties sporting their one
long fill'er-up night on the rice-white silks? And

Morgan, didn't we make our fire? From water,
from air, from the fur and the rind. From antimatter. Fire.
From the shine in the knob on the door at the very shimmybone-end
of the raw blue hallway of nothing. Didn't we
arson its planks? Baby, weren't the banks of the river Body
ablaze, their nerve-tip cattails torched? Baby, didn't we
kindle? Weren't we candescent fleshes? Didn't we burn?
Well, yes. And now here is its urn, and its ashes.

✷ ✷ ✷

Even my ex-wife offered to phone him . . .   One morning, a moment
before sun chutes through his window, I think of the serial
travel of language in "telephone"—the children's game. No matter
their exactitude in repetition, something like *my life is
one of plenty* transforms. The rhino Dürer did
became the rhino all of Europe did, in stages away
from that model, for over two centuries—a 200-year-long
flipbook of the fabulous. Scant changes departing from archetype

—so, evolution. Or film. Imagine a movie
in which each hundredth frame of the reel varies even only
slightly. Given infinity and an opening shot of Tara, we
might still achieve the whole of *Gone with the Wind* . . . Sun
enters, winnowed by blinds, and touches every bedside object,
touches the photo I've placed here—he's a young man,
younger than I am now, and holding me . . . And I whisper
to one, or maybe both, of these fathers of mine, *My wife has*

upped and left me. Now the sun is gilding
everything; along his cheek each stubble catches flame.
A crowd of pilgrims bearing candles. Angels burning
on the plain. In the *Sheet of 1,000 Buddhas* no
two are the same, not really. In one, the nimbus nearly
burnt-out like a bulb. In one, that circle of *satori*-glow
so inky it's a parka-hood. And a Buddha so faintly
stamped on the paper, he seems being eaten by light itself.

✴ ✴ ✴

Pain sleeps around. Pain visits my father and tongues hot
damp fidelities in his ear, and yet I walk the ward and witness
pain hop body to body, sleazetramp, bedjumper,
anyone's for a night. So I was wrong. Pain isn't "insular," it's
held in common. Maybe that's true of joy as well; the village church
and town whore both are meeting-places, after all, I've heard
men speak about in terms of democratic entry even though
the time inside is of necessity a private one. But joy

is for another poem, or other part of this poem. I mean pain.
I mean the irreducible atom of hurt when Jimbo told Yvonne
about his lover we'd all take later to calling The Spider Woman
because of how he danced trapped at the sticky pit of her web . . . I see it
turning, silver, cold, in place
in the horrible center-of-gravity keeping Arlene Bedoya from rising
out of the flesh that remembers and into new flesh fresh
of experience. Brothers; Arlene and Jimbo are brothers, are sisters. One

night, hopeless, I walked miles under a moon like a bit of
mineral spar too small to save the smallest of anyone down here
from drowning in darkness. Walking, over to the lake.
And singing—keening, more like it. A song of soul-
puked-up-the-gullet. Walking, to the line where earth and wave
contended. Walking, alone. And not alone, not truly,
Tony, not ever, Jackie H., conceiving this, planning the stanzas,
walking the edge of everyone's divorce.

The fall shows rerun in summer. / Individual ragged
salmon return up the rungs, squeeze deep of the last of their own
full milt-sacs, shudder, and turn to single bloody-silver
muscles floating the current. And then? / An AM station cycles back
the goldies, and the new songs are the old songs anyway: heartbreak,
heartsublimity. And then? / The legends say Arthur will
return. And Quetzalcoatl, return. And the miracle-speaking
Messiah of the Jews. And then? And then. / My niece of all

of 2½ years, Lindsay Nichol, is driving the whole house fucking
nuts with her day's two new-learned words *supwise!* and *hostabul,*
running them endlessly in and out of her brain's maze
like white lab mice till the lessons are learned past doubt.
Wheh Gwampy? Grampy's sick—remember?—but
we'll let you talk on the phone. And later that evening, at his hostabul
bed, they'll loosen the tubes when the phone rings. Gwampy? Hewwo
supwise! And then? / October: the leaves,

their interior pyrrhic gold-reds. And then. The repetitions. How
they mean a separation. How they mean a tie. / Picasso:
how an ancient Dogon fertility dancer stares through the eyes
of his cubed Cannes bathing beauty. / Halley's comet: a comma
on fire—one of a series. / DNA. / And then? / And always
"and then." And the moon. Then no moon. / "One virtue
exists for the vastest mass of mankind:
Money."—this said by Theógnis, mid-6th century B.C.

✴ ✴ ✴

October: morning. Arlene Bedoya rehearsing her passionate Christmas
wrapping paper and ribbons. Here, I say my own one line,
in my own one mouth, I've never repeated out loud to this man but
aim at his body in silence, send in silence, like a sound wave
from a mute, through where his labyrinthine systems grip
and fail, down the grain of him and its every more-minuscule ripple.
I love you. Morgan's sent a card. He reads it, smiles. She's
x'ed a line of kiss-signs on it, my ex. So now I've been in both

their bodies, in my own way, for a small time, but no matter
whatever connection remains, must go on as and into
myself even longer. When I started this poem, I wanted to say
a true thing, and conclusive. But I see it's only another day
of charts and oxygen, fear and peripheral hope. Old
patients check out, new in. They're wheeling the many moaning
words of the text of our mortality from one ward to another,
bed to bed, like printing, like slugs of movable

type. And of the message Chunosuke Matsuyama
scratched on wood and gave, a last communication, to
the flux . . . ? What are the odds? What are the crazy ineffable units
of sun, of salt? In 1935, it washed up—over 150 years
later—on the beach outside a tiny Japanese fishing village. The
village of his birth. If I rewrite this poem or you reread it, you
out there in the Yonder (yes, reread it: please) leave that small note
of closure in. It's a heartening fact. And then some.

Tarpan and Aurochs

In certain cases, it is possible to recreate extinct animals through careful breeding of present-day species. Two species that have been successfully recreated are a type of wild horse and a prototypical form of cattle.

—The World Almanac Book of the Strange #2

Eventually you'll be called. It will be
over water, or will appear to be
over a great expanse of water, no matter
where you are: the passage will be dark
with just a far, red rind of light that seems
to say an unseen shore. It may not be
a "shore," but water comes to mind, and
fish: some matrix-you, an early time of day
or life: a place that's amniotic. There's something calling
—your name, you think. And you hear it as if
over water. It will happen, and it will happen to you
in just this way. —Your real name, who you were
all along. Hoof-in-the-walking, Horn-from-the-skull,
Small-chain-of-original-protein.

In the subway car, peripheral vision flickers
unexpectedly with the B-train on the next track over
starting up, so giving you that second's (or less) illusion of
backwards travel. Travel backwards,
then: a blurred face in a length of A-train
rewound like a film. Who hasn't once
seen skydivers rise like that, the 'chutes above them
closing like flowers photography's run wrongway, then finally
folding like flowers, compactly back into the seed
—and not imagined himself in the car that tunnels
retrograde through time, to be the string
of metabolic process not yet even hard-wired
into the neural circuits, not yet even fetal REM, for which
midwifery hands are so macroscopic they don't exist.

✷ ✷ ✷

There are paintings in which the souls of men are
breaking out of their bodies and rising like steam
from warm, torn bread, like steam with a very
calm face—and you see the painters really
believed in this, along with gold and rats
it's what the Middle Ages was all about.
The point of view is almost that of the souls'
—the flesh we take for granted, so everything paint
can mean to semblance is given to spirit's
verisimilitude. Finally, looking long enough,
the opposite occurs: it's the bodies of men we need
convincing of—did we really belong
to those things on the ground? (A waft, a spark,
is enough now.) Could such rough husks be ancestral?

✷ ✷ ✷

I said *fetal REM*. The friend of a friend has found
the migratory stopping-place for North America's
monarchs: in the mountains north of Mexico City
37,000,000 drowse in conifers, one dun molecule or two of
thorax-susurration away from not being
anything at all. After sex, a lady asks
how many butterflies one of our heartbeats
could power. I turn to her not even knowing
the width of the border between a man and a woman
—slickness atoms-thick? or something so
large as prehistory and we'll never cross it
in this life? That the fetus's eyelids correspond
to one of those idling butterflies, I know, the way
we all know the travel of light though perhaps not its formula.

⁎ ⁎ ⁎

There's no measure for that distance. —But
you. Eventually you'll be called; you'll go, and be
a standard unit through incredible space. No
I don't want to turn from the pleasures of mattress,
glass, the well-bound book, the well-glazed duck
l'orange with almond slivers, electrical pylon
softened in morning snow, the nylon bunched about
her toes then straightened transparently over a thigh . . .
But we'll be called, so must prepare; must even
understand our hands on rocks, in sun, regress
to lizards; even learn to love the light the way the nuclei
of algae do, entire; even learn to love the dust and
even the subatomic bones of the dust; and make
the tarpan and aurochs, name them, know them eye to eye.

One Continuous Substance

A small boy and a slant of morning light
both exit the last dark trees of this forest, though
the boy is gone in an instant. Not

the light: it travels its famous 186,000 miles per second
to be this still gold bar
on the floor of the darkness. I suppose

that from the universe's point of view
we do the same: a small boy and an old man
being one continuous substance.

We were making love when the phone rang
saying my father was dead, and the sun
kept touching you, there, and there, where I'd been.

Sentimental

The light has traveled unthinkable thousands of miles to be
condensed, recharged, and poured off the white white pages
of an open Bible the country parson holds in front of this couple
in a field, in July, in the sap and the flyswirl of July
in upper Wisconsin, where their vows buzz in a ring in the air
like the flies, and are as sweet as the sap, in these rich and ritual minutes.
Is it sentimental? Oops. And out of that Bible the light continues
to rush as if from a faucet. There will be a piecrust cooling
out of its own few x'ed-out cuts. And will it make us run
for the picklier taste of irony rolled around protectively on our tongues
like a grab of Greek olives? My students and I discuss this
slippery phenomenon. Does "context" matter? Does
"earned" count? If a balled-up fidget of snakes
in the underbrush dies in a freeze is it sentimental? No,
yes, maybe. What if a litter of cocker spaniels? What
if we called them "puppydogs" in the same poem in that same hard,
hammering winter? When my father was buried,
the gray snow in the cemetery was sheet tin. If I said
that? Yes, no, what does "tone" or "history" do
to the Hollywood hack violinists who patiently wait to play
the taut nerves of the closest human body until from that
lush cue alone, the eyes swell moistly, and the griefs
we warehouse daily take advantage of this thinning
of our systems, then the first sloppy gushes begin . . .
Is that "wrong"? Did I tell you the breaths
of the gravediggers puffed out like factorysmoke
as they bent and straightened, bent and straightened,
mechanically? Are wise old (toothless) Black blues singers
sentimental?—"gran'ma"? "country cookin'"? But
they have their validity, don't they, yes? their
sweat-in-the-creases, picking up the lighting
in a fine-lined mesh of what it means to have gone through time
alive a little bit on this planet. Hands shoot up . . . opinions . . .
questions . . . What if the sun wept? the moon? Why, in the face

of those open faces, are we so squeamish? Call out
the crippled girl and her only friend the up-for-sale foal,
and let her tootle her woeful pennywhistle musics.
What if some chichi streetwise junkass from the demimonde
gave forth with the story of orphans forced through howling storm
to the workhouse, letting it swing between the icy-blue
quotation marks of cynicism—*then?* What if
I wept? What if I simply put the page down,
rocked my head in my own folded elbows, forgot
the rest of it all, and wept? What if I stepped into
the light of that page, a burnished and uncompromising
light, and walked back up to his stone a final time,
just that, no drama, and it was so cold,
and the air was so brittle, metal buckled
out song like a bandsaw, and there, from inside me,
where they'd been lost in shame and sophistry
all these years now, every last one of my childhood's
heartwormed puppydogs found its natural voice.

Powers

Whizzer, The Top, Phantasmo . . . They come back sometimes,
now that my father comes back
sometimes. With their lightningbolts sewn
the size of dinner utensils across their chests, with their capes
rayed out, with their blue lamé boots. And he . . . ? It's
hazy, usually; he's a part of that haze. It talcs
his early morning stubble, it muffles the worry
love so often set like candles in his eyes. And: "Albie . . ."/then
that smile meant kindly, but also to say it came from some source
wiser than mine/". . . all this reading is fine. But there's a
real world." It wasn't The Streak. It wasn't Mistress Miracle.
With their antigravity belts, their bellcurve muscles.
Night. One lamp. While he read every scrap of fiscal scribble
that said the rent couldn't be met, and in the darkness
tried to fight that vague opponent with every poor
persuasive scrappy peddler's stratagem he had, I read
by flashlight under the covers: City Hall was being burgled
of its Gems of the World display, and Captain Invincible faced
a Mineral Ray (that already turned 2 bank guards and a porter
into clumsily-rendered crystalline statues) jauntily,
his wisecracks by themselves could make a "mobster" or
that dreaded gorillaish creature in a double-breasted suit,
a mobster's "goon," collapse in the ultimate cowardly self-exposure
of "crooks" and "scoundrels" everywhere. The Dynamo
could will himself into a wielder of electrical jolts, and even
invaders from Alpha-10 were vanquished. Smasheroo's
special power was fists "with the force of entire armies."
Flamegirl was . . . well, flames. And flying,
almost all of them, blazoned on sky—a banner, an imperative
above our muddling lunch-and-shrubbery days.
With their "secret identities": Spectral Boy, who looks like someone's
winter breath (and so can enter "criminal hideouts" through keyholes,
etc.) is "in reality" Matt Poindexter, polo-playing dandy;
The Silver Comet, whose speed is legendary and leaves

small silver smudges on the page as he near-invisibly zips by, is
ironically wheelchair-bound and Army-rejected
high school student and chemistry ace Lane Barker;
The Rocket Avenger parks cars; Celestia is a bosomy
ill-paid secretary. It could happen—couldn't it?—
to me: the thick clouds part as neat as prom-night hair
and a nacreous flask of Planet Nineteen's "wizard elixir" be
beamed down to my bedside: I would wake reciting
a Pledge Against Evil, and set to work designing whatever
emerald star or halo'd eye would be incised on my visor, it
could happen, right?—I wasn't Me but
an inchoate One of Them. With their Wave Transmitter Wristlets,
with their wands, their auras, their cowls. The Insect Master.
Blockbuster. Astro Man. Miss Mystery. Gold Bolt. Solaris . . .
They come back to me now, they ring the bedroom air sometimes
like midges at the one watt of my consciousness, and sleep
is entered with this faint token of sentinel benignity upon me.
Maybe because sleep also
isn't what my father called the "real world." And
he . . . ? Dead
now, with his stone, with his annual candle, my father is
also a fiction. And so he appears
with their right to appear, from the kingdom of the impossible,
he appears in their midst, with Doctor Justice,
The Genie, The Leopardess, Meteor Man . . . he steps out
from that powerpacked crowd, he's thrown his factory outlet jacket
sloppily over his shoulders, it's late, so dark now, and
he's worried about me. Someone may as well be. I'm
in pieces over some new vexation: hopeless in the drizzle,
perhaps, a flashlight clamped abobble in my mouth, and trying to find
    whatever
damage in the mysterious shrieks and greaseways of an engine
bucked me ditchside in the wee hours; or, with equal befuddlement,
staring damp-eyed at the equally damaged wants and generosities
awhirr in the human heart. And: "Albie . . ."/then that very
gentle yet censorious shake of the head/". . . how many times
have I told you? Be patient. Never force your tools or materials.
Don't give up." At moments like this, that his blood

pumps through me, his blood is half of what actually made me, seems
as wondrous as Bob Frank "deep in the jungles of Africa"
dying of fever and being saved by—positively
thriving on—a transfusion of mongoose blood.
This was in 1941, in *USA Comics;* Frank returned to New York
as the Whizzer—superfast, in an outfit
the yellow of mariners' slickers. And Triphammer.
Ghost King. The Scarlet Guardian. Eagleman. Magic Scarab. The
  Wraith.
With their domino masks or their gladiatorial helmets.
The Mighty Elasto. Lady Radiant. Space Devil. Reptile Boy.
With their various signs of legitimacy: their pharaonic rings,
atomic lariats, stun guns, mystic arrows, tridents, with
such amulets as hinge the Earth and Heavens into symbiotic grace.
The Invoker: I remember, he kept two planets at peace. And
  Hydro-Man:
could turn to water (a dubious strength, I always thought) and once
he conducted a current that fried some miscreant, so rescued
a willowy flibbertigibbet princess. And Panther Woman: her golden
  claws
and sinuous inky tail were all the good that (successfully) stood between
a scientist "bent on enslaving the world to his crazed whims" and
the populace of "Center City," the first place on his list. And
Whizzer . . . I remember, once, Whizzer was . . . I put down the page.
The knocking. The landlady. He was shaking
in front of her. She filled the door. He had to explain
the doctor cost extra money this month, and he worked all week
on double shifts, he really did, but this one time
we didn't have the rent, we'd be late, he was fighting back crying,
who'd never had to say such a thing before to such a person.
I remember: he said it straight to her face,
the one good pair of suit pants keeping its crease in the closet
cried but he didn't, the long day's wadded-up tissues cried out,
and the bar sign blinking pinkly across the street,
the horseshoes of dust that collect on the house slippers under the bed,
The Little Taxi That Hurried and *Scuffy the Tugboat,* that sorrily-stained
lame angelwing of an ironing board, the ashtrays and the aspirin,
everything yielded up its softness then,

the carpet was green and black, the light was ruthless,
his voice never broke and his gaze never shifted although
the universe did, because we would be one week late, there! he said it,
he said it clearly, to her and to everyone,
spent, and heroic.

Desire Song

The graspy heart, that lobster of ours that
wants, and wants, and is evolved to lust
for one grain shat by a swallow in flight
as much as the whole packed 4-story silo.
There's a cloud across the moon tonight
like the skin boiled milk gets
cooling—slightly blue and slightly wrinkled.
I want the glass of warm milk from my childhood
carried up to the crib by a living Grandma Nettie
with her hair still singed in odor
from the frightening tines of her old-fashioned curler,
yes, and I want the moon
in its entirety, the moon through the windshield
detailing Phyllis's breast for me the first time
it was more than a wish or a centerfold
peeked in private, yes, I want the moth of faint veins
holding her nipple, the coruscations it made
in stiffening, casting complicated shadows within itself
not unlike the moon, which I want,
and that '63 Chevy we parked in, which I want,
and the father who loaned it to me that night,
who I want waiting up for me, walking the planet
instead of being one more battery slipped inside it,
powering the rest of us, who are sweating our sheets
with our wanting. Michael tells me:
in the slammer—call it what you like, the pen,
the hoosegow, the big house, call it shit city—
you want *anything* from outside, and
a used-up tube of lipstick or the one-eyed spaniel's water pan
can hold the same desire a limousine does.
He's seen kneeling men lick cell bars
for the salt a visitor's palm left.
Think of the ribcage . . . think of the lobster
clacking inside its trap.

The World Trade Center

Miss Cherry Harvest of 1954 is savvily bing-bedecked
in snug red mounds of endorsement. Miss Home Hardware
overflows a gray bikini-top (done as a wingnut). Miss
Asbestos Insulation. Miss Kosher Franks. The Aluminum
Siding Queen of 1957. "I was never so completely
cherished, or so much a dispensary of happiness, as that
night distributing candy samples and wearing the fabulous
sack that said REFINED, Miss Sugar Industry always wore . . ."
In jade: Miss Lawn Fertilizer, a weedy fringe
over her goodies. In gold: Miss Beer of the Year. "I was never
so debased. All night, this gross parade of paunchy gawkers
asking to eat my donuts, or punch the holes out
of my donuts, or use their cream in my donuts, or put their
nuts on my donuts. Thirty years later I hate those people
still. And donuts." Miss New Paper Goods
in marbled corrugation. The Bow-and-Arrow-Fair Queen.
Miss Kitchen Appliances waving like the Pope, though with
a greater sartorial splendor than the Pope's, from her silverized
pedestal at the heart of an 8-foot facsimile blender and
when it's on, she pirouettes in facsimile of its power and speed.
The Cupcake Girl. The Hog By-Products Lady of 1962. We
need to love them. If every present moment is only a choice
some moment planted in the past made, then we need to love
these seeds of us if we're to love ourselves. Miss
Railroad Boxcars doing her choo-choo shuffle,
Miss Poultry, Miss Dry Ice. And little foil-petaled
nougat-and-marshmallow come-ons for the kiddies. One
free packet of cleanser. A complimentary photo of yourself
agog in the per-hour arms of Miss Pool-and-Patio Barbeque
while her court of attendant Charcoal Briquettes in their smokey hose
and baggy ash-like swimsuits dances in back. We
need to condemn them. This is the clownshow, this is the horribly
misshaped idea of sex's functions, and this
is the wedding of physical loveliness with commerce, we

contain as possibilities, let bloom sometimes and
need to root out. Miss Midwest Pharmaceuticals Co-op.
Need to refute. To look at us looking at Miss
Electric Handtools Festival looking at herself,
and gag. "I loved the attention, I loved making everyone feel
good, and nobody took it too seriously, it was fun just
like a mardi gras, and why not, I guess you can say,
well, I loved it." Miss Home Furnishings bouncing her bosomy
sponsorship of "Comfort *plus* Affordability" to and fro on the
bosomy couch. Miss Styrofoam. Miss Nuclear Power.
"I'd drag home dangling trains of plastic pretzels
off my fanny, so humiliating, and after a night of stinking drunk
tycoons and their yes-men downing slabs of sirloin and champagne
I'd open the door on my mother feeding on tea and breadcrusts and
I'd slam down my lousy day's wage." Miss Phone of the Future.
Miss Potato Crop of 1959. "A lot of care went into it,
all of the papier-mâché croissants and bagels they sewed on, and all
of the themesong lyrics, which I helped with" (sings:) "I'm the Bakery
Queeeeen with the tender lovin' oven" (now a faraway glazed look
in her eyes:) "I'll
never be that alive again." Miss American Plumbing. Miss
Sporting Goods. We must look at them closely, every
lipsticked mouth a beet-red butterfly quivering over hilly
fields of décolletage. The Lingerie and Sleepwear Queen.
Miss Fireproof Camping Gear. Miss Lumber Exposition. We
must look at them wholly, culture-wide, cross-time, like flowers
in speeded film, so many gauzy tutus being donned and doffed
a day—if these are flowers relegated to another age
by evolution, still we need to preserve their most exquisite sherbet
    pastels
and their greatest butchercolor striations. Vibrant
delegates of their mute, assigned constituency: wood paneling,
doorknobs, freestone peaches, tractor tires, picnicware.
Miss Pet Food. Miss Circus Equipment. Miss Pickle of
1957, '58, '59, and '60. And where are you now,
Miss-Pickle-handing-out-gherkin-slices, the welter
of seagreen spinach-and-celadon confetti long swept away, and where
are you now, Miss Carpet Shampooing Institute, now what

doting grandmama or business mafiosa have you been
borne to by the rising tide of that yesteryear's foamy bubbles?
I mean it. People die, and these traces remaining
pain us, Miss Furs, Miss Radio Home Repair—where
did your idling taxi finally breeze you afterwards, and
what became of that 10-year-old in the thick black glasses
watching you whisk grotesquely but ineffably away
until his father said "Albert it's late" then they left too
and what's become of the one in his grave and the other becoming
the age of the one, Miss Memory-Up-In-A-Puff,
Miss First-Wet-Kiss-With-Its-Glory-And-Shame, Miss
Lexicon-Of-Woe, Miss Poetry-Firing-Over-The-Skin, Miss Confusion,
Miss Needlepoint Maxims, Miss Funeral Shovel, Miss Semenburst,
Miss Everything, Miss Spider-Of-Blood-In-Its-Bodywide-Web.
We hate you. We're telling you now: we're ashamed,
Miss Amalgamated Canning Concerns, Miss Taxidermy, Miss
Soybean Dealers. Miss Generating Stations with the tiara
of flashing lightbulbs in your platinum hair. Miss Guilt.
Miss Undeniably Breathtaking Tenderness. Miss Knife-and-Gun.
We value you, with incredible passion. Miss Loosened Burnoose
in the Deepening Desert Sunset, Miss Tonsils, Miss Lesbian Love,
Miss Verdigris Glimmering Beautifully On A Hull Though No One
    Sees It,
Miss Guava Bushelboys Of The Tropics, Miss Beef, we want you,
come nearer, be ours, Miss Manmade Fibers, Miss Avocado, Miss
Charge-Built-Up-About-A-Lightning-Rod-Like-A-Vigorous-
Sweetheart-Imagined-Around-The-Dildo, Miss Penance,
Miss Tallow, Miss Fossil, Miss Radium Technology, come
hither, where are you, what's happened to almost everyone
we know, do you remember us from that evening
in the fog we'd bring like intermittent patches of forgetfulness
for the rest of our lives and our seeking, tell us. Do you
miss us? Miss Us. Miss You.

Spies (Spies? Spies.)

1.

are everywhere. / They float,
trenchcoated, slant-capped, from deep cover and code name
into the always unsatisfactory half-revelation
of newspaper headlines. / Ultrasound
sweeps deepness for the human fetus
and Nessie impartially. / First the serpent
reconnoiters Eve—then,
civilizations later, a microtransmitter planted inside
a martini olive reports some woman's pillow-natter
directly to HQ. / Espionage
of telescope and stars, of information-tweezing
priest and confessee, of bug-eyed girl on her knees
at the stark-lit crack in the bathroom door
one night as daddy pees . . . / Let's spy
on me: I'm

* * *

7, peering under the ever-braiding skin
of Humboldt Creek and, farther on, the calm
and glutted pond it ruffles into. A duo of chipmunks
cavorts nearby; but I'm near-mesmerized
by the subsurface gulpings of great
handbag-sized fish, as if the car keys,
a kerchief, torn concert tickets, just might
leisurely spiral from those throats and spell
some secret life to the air. Was I
a "spy"? No. Was this "wrong"? No. Though
if I swiveled that same observation 180
degrees, sneak-peeking the hot-stuff couple
grazing each other's necks on a shadowy
park bench—*then?* Was Nixon's

wiretapping "wrong"? He "meant well." Meaning
—what? When I was 17

my father would wait, however long it lasted,
3 in the morning, 4, until my date
(she drove, I didn't yet) pulled softly under
the block's most lushly canopied tree
for a last goofy passionate smooch: and out
of love? concern? sheer nosiness? his
wakeful sentinel eye would burn
from a chink in the livingroom blinds straight
into my teenage brain's overwary
embarrassment center. We'd argue. I'd tell him go
to hell. I'm 41 now, *that's*
what I'm embarrassed over. Yes: it *was* his own
lonely version of love, I think. But
love for me in those crazy hormonal days meant
walking into the house with a fresh fishy smear
of my girlfriend over my mouth—from,
as she'd say (embarrassed
but knowing her needs and their empetaled location)
"down there." Well, that was fine with me,
a novice, a supplicant, someone exploring the mysteries
finely creased in places "down there" even she couldn't guess at yet
—a spy in the valley of love.

2.

The vagina of O'Keeffe's
Grey Line with Black, Blue, and Yellow
is also a flower's
infinitely receding tissuey layers. It's wet
still, done, redone, on one of two easels
this morning in 1953 in Abiquiu. She
studies this painted image—not for content so much
right now, but its overall shape on the canvas.
Beside it, another canvas, with the same shape, but:

a horse skull. She flicks
back and forth and back and forth, while desert light
acts as an awl in her studio, scraping everything
free of the inessential. She's studying likeness
and layers: an espionage of what
ticks at the quick of us. It reminds me of
the Sung Dynasty poet Chiant Te-li's two lines:
Painting plum blossoms is done like judging horses
—By bone-structure, not by appearance.

✦ ✦ ✦

It reminds the informer
—a "confidential informant of Bureau-proven reliability,"
according to the file—of nothing, duty and bile
blocking anything other than damning-by-implication
reportage: that she "made remarks
which would not be made by a loyal American,"
that "she frequently entertains guests of foreign extraction,"
one even "appeared to be either Chinese or Filipino
and did not speak any English . . ." 1953, and O'Keeffe
is under surveillance
for the FBI office in Albuquerque. A "mail watch"
is placed on her correspondence. Her observer somehow
scrutinizes her bookshelves. Altogether,
117 pages of dossier are amassed toward no particular end
by Hoover's snooping boys. For Dorothy Parker,
1,000 pages. Theodore Dreiser, 240.
Archibald MacLeish, 600+ . . .
The ear against the tapestry of a medieval council-of-war,
and the spy jet thermalphotographing missile installations:
each has its own sensibility, but
I see them as two of endless circles around her
passionate daubing of paint, up to her elbows
in coral, turquoise, burnt sienna, terra verde, dove-gray, amethyst,
    ocher . . .
1953. The orbits of the atom build up
to the rings of the onion, and these are like

the pearly bands in the universe-wall that oversee
the Music of the Spheres; they revolve; and,
surreptitiously, each watches each.

★. ★. ★.

Those two "cavorting chipmunks" . . . ?—mechanical
transmission devices, disguised as living things.
If I unreel their tapes and play back
1955, I see that curious 7-year-old boy being led home
hand in hand, by his curious father. I can even
feel the finger bones in the older one's hand, see?, playing
with the slippery give of knuckle-skin over the knuckles.
And if I follow the tape up
30 more years, I'm cradling his head in my arms
the week before he dies, I'm feeling the hardness
under the delicate skin at the temples, I'm rubbing
pressure-points against the unavoidable skull. O'Keeffe
would understand. But who can understand
those moments when he still appears
over my shoulder now, a sentient
smudge on the oxygen, and noting,
as if they were meaningful, the very confused
particulars of my life? It's like
old times, in a way. It's his own
lonely version of love, I think. The air
goes cloudy . . . I feel his gaze . . .
Who does he report to?

The Dynamics of Huh

*The drummers of the Lokele who live in the jungle of
Zaire, not far from the former Congo River, still know
the sayings that fit their tom-tom rhythms. In fact they
need the sayings in order to drum the rhythms. But no
one now remembers what they mean—or whether they
ever "said" anything.*

—ILLICH AND SANDERS
in *ABC*

I can't begin to guess the contents of these U-Haul moving cartons
someone's dumped in a rush, abandoned in this gutter, but the pure
dumb blocky form of it is so eloquent of those few
yet truly hellish address-hopping years that followed the divorce
—assembling each new stinking retinue of cardboard flats
and wrapping, endlessly, wrapping until some first grayish dribble
of dawn, then wrapping more—that a column of heebie-jeebies,
like fire ants, rampages my spine. Or the 21st Indian

Intertribal Pow-Wow moaning soulfully out of the TV is
that box's incomprehensible substance—war?
peace? rain? it's obdurate Extraterrestrial to me—and even
so, this solemn ululating, in the way it ceremonially
assumes the human heart and godly ear connect, and
wrings a little blood, a little blood with wings, for the one
to be heard by the other . . . in this, it brings
completely back to me the old Jews on their New Year

in the willfully uncomfortable storefront Orthodox *shul*
my father favored when I was 10 or 11 and watching them
softly rock their prayer as if each slowdanced in place
with an angel, and listening as their opaque wall of Hebrew,
uttered brick by brick, rose out of the room to somewhere
I could never believe and they could never not. When I was
10, the common comic-book expression "Huh?"
might have stood for whole days of my life; once,

in that room where the apartment bulged enough
for the indulgence of an extra secondhand sofa—they called it
the sunroom—I came on my father weeping, my father
turning his wide face physically inside-out
by tears. I remember: the light, and the lace drapes, placed
a wavy veil over his eyes. And all he said
of it then or would ever say was just *One day
you'll understand,* words wobbly and much furzed-over. Well, one day

has come and gone, or maybe one day's really everyday eventually.
I've waked to see the woman beside me finely designed
along her upthrust haunch by sleepcreases
hieroglyphically alien, and evocative
of the whole encoded beings we are in the whole contextual
dazzling unbreakable code of social knottedness and night sky
we inherit. In a world like that, an insomniac man might
walk although it rains, although the Pow-Wow thousands

prayed all day for rain. He stops: the downpour's softened
the U-Haul boxes. As he looks, one fist of water sloshes through,
then opens, bearing a wickedly metal-studded leather corset,
a child's party hat with a paper spray of what seem cockatoo
rump-feathers, and a fraying plum-velvet New Testament he
nabs and finds inscribed with the names of 3 generations
in English, Finnish, and Arabic. Huh? It makes me
want to call my father, across the layers of shale,

worm-warren, and motherlode coal that separate us,
offering my much-thumbed Life/Death dictionary
so we can speak, and telling him simply how deeply I *know*
so much now, but I can't *understand.*

How the World Works: An Essay

That's my topic. How complex, Alhambran arabesques of weather
(seen computer-screened by satellites); and the weathering eddies on tiles
in the courtyards and intimate tryst-rooms and policy chambers
of the Alhambra itself: construe a grander pattern.
How the west wind whipples the osiers. How the slivery, eyeless
cave fish in Mexico slip through their fissures unerring.
In Nepal, a poacher reams a spoonful of musk
from that orifice near the urethra, holding—with his other
gloved hand—the deer's small death-kicks steady; and in
mid-Manhattan at 3 A.M., at Chico's place, the Pimp Prince
enters swimming in coke, with one new frou-frou dewy-cunted
acolyte on each eelskin sleeve, and he reeks of a vial
of musk. I'm singing the rings-in-rings song of the planet,
its milks, its furnaces, its chlorophyll links. One

suddenly clear blue afternoon (when I was 8) of the kind
Lake Michigan unhoards at winter's thinner end,
the sky: a child soprano's pure high-C struck after
months of ugly gutturals . . . a copper (as my father still
referred to them), a copper of the old school, beefy, easy, from
the one-foot-on-the-runningboard days of Chicago ticketdom,
stopped us *slam* in the midst of our shoreline spree, the flasher
calling all of Heaven's attention, I thought, to this misfortunate
secondhand dent-bodied Chevy. "Officer, have you had
breakfast?" "Why, no sir." And he wetted his finger and thumb
(he always did this with money) and from (as my father
still called a wallet) his billfold, a 5 (you could do it for 5
in those days) sleeked on over. Later, educative and high on this
his mastery, he winked and told me that was how the world

worked. This was part of an interlocked system for him as
sure as the ecoconnectedness in the italic stance of a cattle egret,
the living shoulders it tweezes, lice that graze this egret's
feather-flesh, and dungbugs shitting the bull's more generous
shit back incremental and rich to the grasses . . . all
neat, clean, a perfect processional circle of textbook arrows.
So: you invited "the Boss" to dinner and used
the holiday silver and chortled at jokes which
were "a riot," and thus you "advanced"; you shmoozed
the waitress, and her service upgraded. This was a very clear
flow chart, and I sing the song of its unctious functioning-well.
I was 8: I believed him. He believed himself. For
thousands of years, for that matter, the planet revolved
Ptolemaically, managing beautifully, thank you. Once

a woman I knew in my days of believing repeated sex
meant knowing a person, said, from out of some vaporous cranial
nowhere, "Do you think we come from monkeys, or little
enemas in the water?" and after the ripplings of pity and comedy
through me, I began the task of explaining the planet: I still
have the cocktail napkin that cartoonily shows Earth
axis-spit and pivoting, and that crudely rules a B.C./A.D. timeline.
This was long ago; I'd like to apologize, now, for that
initial pity: once I saw the tiny beads of bravery she needed
to restring each morning just to face the next
dyslexic day, I understood—too late to do love any good—
the shadows she walked through the rest of us didn't. And
by then of course I'd also come to understand my father
wasn't sharp or slick but small in a way

that makes me tender toward him: one more anyone
with his salesman's satchel, and son, and wife, like counters
in some global game, "Advantage," tycoons and brigadiers play. Well
now he's *in* the globe, beyond maneuvering. I saw him
lowered; now he's part of the parfait striations I'm singing of,
part of the nitrogen/flywheel/hovel-and-palace totalityworks
called Terra—where the butterfly fish
at mating time, the vivid-hued and specifically-patterned
butterfly fish, fights rivals with its colors for weapons,
its cinnabars and its veridians, deepening, quivering, them . . .
while out back of Chico's, the Pimp Prince stands
his gaudy ground in front of a would-be usurper,
plumed hats, ostrich boots, gold neckchains,
one a ruby ring, one jade . . . Oh the world

not only works but networks, rarefiedly, in
topnotch geewhillikers form. The ever-ravenous protozoa
in the rumen-goop of that bull I earlier mentioned, burbling
away at their cellulose walls . . . by one hashbrowns-surrounded
breakfast steak, they *are* connected to some soul-weary
salesman in 1929 pulling in to a roadside diner architected to be a
giant coffee pot on Pacific Highway outside South Tacoma.
Let the sign of that connection be the thready, heady
olfactory-waft of ant saliva the anteater rides like radar
unto its repast. And so there *is* a mode, an almost diagrammable
order, albeit on levels sub and supra while we sit around
in the dark with our luminous human desires confusing the
everything that they're a part of. Still we need
to remember, against our own small breakdown days. Once

after my father had died but before the family car was sold
I joyrode with a lady, one-handed wheeling us up
the curves past Lighthouse Point. A cop clocked our speed:
an hour later I was in custody—a shabby, crapped-up,
roach-infested custody—for attempting to bribe. It was
bad, but I was good, and it was brief. What's longer and
sticks with me more is being dropped off back at the car,
too tired even to feel defeated, somewhere on damp sand
miles from anywhere 3 or 4 in the morning. When
the engine wouldn't turn, that last indignity, all I could do
was sit stupidly humming—not singing just humming—
on the hood, and stare at the first gray rhythmic swashing
in-and-out of the water, sure that nothing ever does, or
ever had really, or ever would, work.

Collecting: An Essay

for Barbara & David Clewell

In the "fuckee bars" of that Oriental city, floor girls
sweep up after the sets with brooms maneuvered by their
beautifully bamboo and nearly hairless you-know-whats,
says Brady. And Brady says the great cathedrals of Europe are
easily rivaled by the architecture of waterfalls that yearly
freeze in the northern passes: minerals from the rock
have dyed those crystalline buttresses, domes, and rose windows
beatitude's colors, orchids and peacocks the lackluster
saints of stone would trade their longevity for—says
Brady. Brady's been a first-rank courier, the world

his office. One day a timelocked lacquer box of diamonds
to Nepal. Again, a set of "security-sensitive" directives
to a pair of silent bison-shouldered sunglassed "contact
deputies" in the sunken gardens of Rome. And the Company
pays for rests between: a week at the black-sand beach where
Brady looks like a pearl shrimp curled on a damp dune of caviar
(where, he says, he diddley-deed with an incognito countess and her
sweetcream-bosomed femme de chambre)—or once a series
of lectures on "Postmodernist Cuisine" at the Sorbonne. Collecting
is passion; these are some of the stories in Brady's album. Here,

today at the West End Weekly Flea, the pleasure is seeing
that same delight in acquisitions's intimate details settle to, and fit,
a stamp (one savvy haggler, 10, is zeroing in on a coveted
Smokey the Bear first-day-of-issue envelope showing
the bruin's gently admonishing visage staring ghostly
from a teal-blue fog) or one of the early 19th century butter molds
this woman with the beaky nose and moleskin collar seeks
and stores and knows by pattern better than most of us
know our own birthmarked skin: palmettoes, looped ivy,
webbing, escutcheony pineapples, cockatoos, rings-in-rings . . . I've seen

Babs bop down the pea gravel aisles in quest of fifties ceramics
with avidity that said by study and awe her very
red blood cells had taken on the vaguely amoebaish/boomerang
look of those wares; and Dave upscrutinizing snaggled cairns
of curios (bisque flappers and their beaus, time-rainbowed
bottles, scrimshaw humidors, a family of tux-and-top-hat
ducks whose scarlet derrieres are flower pots . . .) in search
of flying saucerania: everything from books of first-hand sightings
to those ashtrays (only squintily reminiscent of some Mother Ship)
he seizes with such discoverer's joy he looks more

otherworldly, whooping, beaming, than his Moonmen finally might.
I use their real names, and these are friends of mine. And I
belabor that because of the others, sharpster
sharkeye-guys and eel-ladies, you'll see slinking those same
democratic rows of bakelite mermaid pins and snuff tins but
with oozy markup and resale charging their hearts—which
is the spark of a battery different from love's, completely.
Babs, however, wouldn't merchandize one crappy plastic nut tray
in the pinch-waisted shape of a hula cutie, once her eye
has cherished it and fastened it connubially

near a zoot-suited spaceman of Dave's. She
renews the inflatable lobster, pig and bee; he keeps the working
1940s windup jug band working. So these objects
are the nuclei in a body of viable love. The rubber
Paddy the Penguin figurine, the poodle lamps, the loosely
oviform goldspecked aqua-trim formica end tables . . . "Albert,
if you ever see a near-mint Paddy the Penguin set of coasters . . ." or
posters or toasters or whateverthehell—they're
collecting. They're bricking their love in safe. They're
whipping themselves exquisitely toward completion. Mo,

the Mickey King of St. Louis, once ushered me upstairs from the shop
to his exemplary sanctum—everywhere, rare avatars of
the Mouse: as lavishly stashed as Vatican treasures, were
the 1935 Mickey and Minnie "play-me-piano," the legendary
target game with the classic "pie-eyed" Mickey cheerfully bearing
the circle with 1000 points, of course the entire Mickey
circus train with prank-playing anthroanimal entourage,
et-endlessly-cetera, saved from time's indiscriminate ferret teeth,
display-cased as if the fate of the cosmos always rested on one
human being's accepting one task with devotion. For me, those

were the Judith Months: I wanted love conducting
efficaciously between two cities so damn much, my psyche
must have been raised in raffia-texture rashes of
hope and effort. Every day was only good material
for a letter to her, every night was overlaying her face
on the bodies of whackoff fancies—trying, as if Eros were
a god who might be wheedled by endurance.
I see now it couldn't flower—that takes soil more
than air. But then, those months, I thought that I could live on air
if she'd write back. And Mo's whole shelfdom told me

people's souls are said by their private devices.
What, doesn't matter—it's how. Whatever rich
collecting I did of that woman in my dreams, I do think
however I did it was right, and signaled something
of consummate care—she'd say the same of herself
and I'd let her. Yes, and so somebody's rummaging
turn-of-the-century ice cream scoops, and somebody Edison
patented gramophone cylinders, and somebody each intact Buck
Rogers raygun and an arsenal of ripoff zip- and zowie-
guns competitors peddled by thousands. I know: "you

can't take it with you." Not one pissant inch of pharaonic lapis
has, so far as we know, materialized amid the Eternal
Lotus Fields there on the Other Side. The tomb is no transport dock.
But sometimes I see this: I'm 7, up late with a cough and
playing in the basement, in the murkily aquarium-like light
sliding off of the battered pea-green office files. My father,
Old Man of a Hundred Woes and Integrities, is groaning. He's put
in another 12 heel-depleting hours hefting his records-book up
the back porch stairs of Cicero, Illinois—for pennies, sweating
cheap-valise insurance shlep that he is, collecting,

collecting. For Metropolitan Life—collecting. And
now that 10 P.M. should see him upstairs, healed in Fannie's arms of
everything deplorable about pitching a company line while dealing
honestly with clients, Mrs.-Koszhkie-of-the-one-eye,
Mr.-Blood-in-his-Handkerchiefopolous . . . here my
father is, math-addled, needing to get the day's
sums straight, and they won't, and the stinking rent and grocery
angst is on him. How I wish now I'd looked up
from coloring Mickey and Donald strictly inside the lines, and
known enough to tell him: even though the columns didn't, something

added up—it was (more, even than numbers)
what counted. Do we ever see that at 7?—how love can be
spoken although in disguise. At 37 I was standing
at his graveside with the mourner's *kaddish* standing
in its many black boots on my tongue. The Hebrew means
the Earth and Heavens should accept their respective percentage
of what his total was at last. And now at last
the living could say their love without embarrassment, nakedly.
(Judith, why can't we ever learn from such moments?) And
the rabbi said, in his words, this—which I give you now in mine:

"At the Gates a man shall be opened and his contents weighed.
Below, the wife she weepeth, and the son he stumbleth
clenched-up through the ritual farewells, yet above,
at the Gates, there is no shadow, for there is no solid object
anywhere to hinder light, and in such light a man is
valued by the being he bears and is, and so with Irving; and
it shall all be canceled stamps, and it shall all be
molded butter, and we shall all be couriers, hearken
to this, no not for caskets of jewels, and not fiestaware, but
a man is a message and we shall all be couriers, verily,

I say unto you: at the end, all of us—couriers."

(Etymologically) "Work Work"

1. Go-Part

Somebody's stuffing excelsior into the penis
of the museum's model aurochs. Somebody's snapping
hundreds of plastic halos into the ruffs of hundreds
of plastic Infants of Prague. Somebody's grading exams.
Somebody's sleeping with the Senator. And
the Senator's promising even more jobs,
more automobile assembly lines, and everything
that means to an edgy electorate. In the kitchen
tonight, my niece is also putting a car together,
out of equal amounts of concentration and crayon.
"This is the go-part here"—the steering wheel,
obviously. Green by black by red, it takes shape.
And orange hubcaps. She's chewing her lip.
She's driven all night by this labor.

2. Shahzzut & Tyupat

Eno's fingers seem as fat as those Red Hot Mama sausages
suspended in brine in a gallon jar, but under my hood
they tweeze out various ailing gobs with the finicky quickness
of surgical pincers. He lifts some oily puzzle-piece into the equally
oily light of the shop, as if it might explain
gravity or antimatter. "Shahzzut," he explains to me, "tyupat,"
in the secret fraternal language of auto mechanics. He
sings to himself: no one has ever been so happy. He's
fixing my engine, he sings, he's polishing my shahzzut
as if it's the milktooth of a saint. "Man's work,
whatever its ostensible purpose, is, at any given time,
to sustain the universe." Tribals, "asked the reason
for ceremony X, say that if they missed one year,
cosmos, the world, would collapse." (Richard Grossinger)

3. Elementary

They weren't handed masks, no one knows why.
We're a pile of elements. No one knows why
they weren't handed masks: they were handed
their slop-poles, though. They were handed the poles
and ordered up the inside catwalk, three stories high.
We're a pile of dirt-cheap elements. They
were ordered up the catwalk, they were told to skim
the floating layer of fester off the top of this
three-story drum of byproducts animal blood.
They weren't handed masks. The drum was 103 degrees.
And one was found face-up and one face-down,
caked into the fester by noon.
We're a pile of dirt-cheap elements, bought,
and toyed with, then tossed with the rest of the shit.

4. Easy Enough

In his book explaining quantum physics John Gribbin
writes, "It is easy enough for me to say 'Anderson measured
the curvature of particle trails and found positrons';
it was much harder for him to do the work." All week
that mundane phrase has hummed itself inside my head
like an abracadabra, conjuring up my father, alive
again, and in the makeshift basement workroom
each night totaling those colossal rows of figures in his war
against an enemy alliance: Rent and Food and Clothes.
It's easy enough for me to wring the sweet rag of nostalgia,
now that he's cold dark particle trails himself.
It's easy enough to ennoble him down there: adding,
juggling, adding, with the same bit lip
his granddaughter later inherited. *To do the work.*

5. Fred: One

That summer (I was seventeen), the powers of Midwest Mercantile
(Roosevelt Road at Jefferson), seeing my reedy body was no use
shlepping delivery crates, assigned me to Accounting, where
my reedy mind was more disastrous yet: I doubt if four
consecutive numbers fit true. One day in the wake
of a contretemps (with tire jacks and a boot-knife)
at the loading dock, Koenig was canned. Would I
pitch in?—meant tussling one unbudgeable sumo
of a crate in the unbearable sun and stares out there,
and just as I was believing death was preferable,
Fred Nelson (The Black Bull everyone called him) moped
on by, in one hand lifted my butt by my belt *and*
in the other the crate, then carried us both the length of the store
and set us like eggs on the top shelf in Wholesale Drapes.

6. Fred: Two

In August, Teaberry Polk—a sassy lassie
from the mending room, whose rump thumpthumped in walking
like a pair of bongos—married Fred Nelson. I don't know what
he did or didn't do, if anything, but on the honeymoon night she
went at his clothes in the closet with a kitchen knife, wildly first, and
then methodically, until his sharkskin suits and French-cuffed shirts
were a wall of ribbon, like some avant-garde "art project." Frankly,
I wish my old friend D. had been upfront like that
with my old friend Jack; instead, it was a long-drawn mess
of misread cues, with kids and sanctimonious tears: the acrimony,
alimony, lawyermoney scene. As for my own divorce
—I remember my mother shaking her head. "Oh Albert . . ."
knowing the heart too needs to be a practiced economy
". . . love, shmove. You have to *work* at it."

7. A Social Section

Begging for work. (An out-of-work worker.)
Begging—for work. (A beggar, "working.") Hat out trusting
in coins: and yes we like this one, but not his beggar brother
faking blindness; or the one who pushes this perimeter further,
sneaking purses; or the one so far he's past this
social seventh section, out of the frame of understandable
reference almost completely: slinking shadow to shadow
with hatchet-edge glint. The feral labor living beyond
/and off/ the labor of civilized lives. The drive home
and the back door jimmied. The girlygirl
peddling her honeyspread under "the viaduck" and why
the hell not?—her man be drown this last week
in a drum of blood at the rendering works. Somebody
profiting off this, somebody buying the Senator lunch, sssh.

8. Brewing

Of a favorite labor in literature I sing. Of Miss
Amelia Edwards, Londoner, braving savagery, vast sands,
and not a little of the alien dyspepsia, to the mountains
of Abu Simbel, the two Great Temples there
with their friezes and carven Colossi. It's 1883. It's
unthinkably ancient and new and amazing.
Her work crew ably swabs the face of the northernmost Colossus,
Ramses II, restoring its whitened splotches with coffee,
"swarming all over the huge head . . . Reïs Hassan
artistically touching up a gigantic nose
almost as long as himself. Our cook stood aghast.
Never before had he been called upon to provide
for a guest whose mouth measured three-and-one-half feet . . .
Ramses' appetite for coffee was prodigious."

9. Bonding

What did I understand? Let's say I was five,
let's say it was Friday, he was bringing me
on the collection route, his salesman smile
in place like a sew-on bowling patch.
The dirty life-cycle of any dollar bill—did I know?
The wheedling and two-bit genuflecting he needed me to see
as professional courtesy—did I see? Did it "take,"
this day of belabored bonding? Was I wiser now?
Time's work is continental drift and the red-shift.
"Opera," "racketeering," "telecommunications"
—workworkwork. On the way home he thumbed a spare coin
at the upturned snap-brim hat of the harmonica beggar
we liked. "So play me a czardas." Well, *sort of* a czardas.
Wheeling me under the skeleton-knocking thunder of the rush-hour el.

10. *Easy Enough*

It's easy enough for me to wring the sweet rag of nostalgia
—not that bucketsful would make a difference now—
or diddle away at the self-set tasks of the poet:
~~planet-shaking~~ skeleton-knocking. "Oh, I've worked *hard*
before this, I once set lobster traps," you always hear
at poetry conventions, "but *nothing's* as difficult as
Selecting The Proper Word!" which is usually just bullshit,
such a bullshit it's not even *real* bullshit, which
weighs down a shovel until the trapezoids scream.
My buddy John once spent a summer hauling cattle,
including hosing the walls of their holding hangar
free of crusted draperies of shit. He did a stint
once in the winter too, and outside of Denver hammered
urine icicles off their pizzle-tips.

11. *The Modes*

Someone busy lawyering: she's torte, she's court,
she's paving over the planet with paperwork justice.
Someone pretending to play a plastic sax with her twat.
The modes of what we call earning a living are the deepness
of the universe in human compactness, and some of it altogether
free of wages: the tomb of the Prophet at Medina was cleaned of dust
by an elder "celebrated for piety and purity" who was lowered
"through a hole in the roof by cords, with directions to wipe it
with his beard" (Sir Richard Francis Burton). *That's*
the work for me! The work for me, each me believes, is
something like being beamed into a spaceship: instantaneous,
acorporeal. But "even angels," says John Donne,
"who are winged, yet had a ladder to go to heaven
by steps"—so, no, there's never an end to it.

12. An End to It

After he retired, after his trophy shelf of crummy
name-plaqued paperweights for *Sales Leader, 19(blahdeblah)*
was plastic'ed-over to keep it free of dust, my father
took up part-time work at a local Shop-Rite,
for minimum wage. He greeted streams of strangers
at the door with that smile he'd used for Metropolitan Life
for thirty-five years and couldn't retire off his face.
The rent wasn't really a problem now—my sister and I
were self-supporting —but every night he returned
to those heavy ledgers in the basement, they were *this*
world's Torah and bore repeated scrutiny, they were a way
of life, were *his* life. When they weren't, one day, he
closed the Book of Life with a slam the nurse's stethescope
heard, and let them do as they pleased with his smile.

13. A Survey

My sister in labor. Labor unions.
Labor law. We can never escape it. The body
asleep is a bellows and a steadily hammered forge.
(Herakleitos: "Even sleepers are doing the world's
work, moving it along a little.") Labor-
atory. So "lab work" comes from (etymologically)
"work work." Skyler earned her pay as a med tech
for a few years; in the lab they had a machine
that shook up cans of patients' shit like one of those
automatic paint can mixers, and one day a can
with too much gas exploded. You can imagine.
The stories! Alice the microbiologist.
Claudia posing nude. My Uncle Lou one evening suddenly
losing his left thumb to the bandsaw.

14. *Over and Out*

Jack calls from Dallas. He says that city's
crime rate is the highest in the country and
last night his ex-wife saw three shadows
slink from a shadow, then enter another shadow,
waiting. Nothing happened—to her,
but this morning the papers are selling a woman's body
chopped in two. "I went to a pawn shop,
I bought a shotgun." It's something like
a 14-gauge or a 22-gauge—I know nothing about these
arsenal terms, to me it's all statistics
from the dark side of the moon. "So that's protection
aplenty?" I venture. He pumps it. My phone fills
with the sound of an Exxon oil tanker cracking in half.
"Oh it'll do the job," he says.

The Poem of the Praises

My name isn't Lucius; I never grew up
to own the mill down at Spiritwood, where the falls makes the river a
    blue leg
slipping into the long white laces of a *danseuse;*
where the marl pit is, and the radiant amber and ember-red wildflowers
like powers, thrones, and dominions putting on bearable form; I
never consolidated with Midas Mill Distribution, and contracted
later with Yancy Hobbs for the stream of half-price darkie sackers,
and later still negotiated the first use of the Edison illuminatory bulbs
in a 3-county area; and one day I didn't think of all the days,
and run into the meadow rubbing my face in the faces of flowers
like a rooting swine until someone came to speak carefully to me and
    carry me home.
My name isn't Rebecca; I never bore three children,
of which Matthew died of the yellow phlegm while still at my nipple,
but Columbine is a poetess of renown and my sweet Lionel Alexander
is the governor's aide; I didn't enter Henry's study
while he was at cards, and open the book of that jackanapes rascal
Darwin as Henry referred to him, and finish the book, and form
my own opinions; I didn't color my conversation with these
while serving the tea, for years, a deep brown veritable
Ganges of tea, and its steamy, pervasive weather; I never
bled, at my "time"; I never crocheted; I never rode Heat Lightnin'.
My name isn't Nathan Lee; I never gave up
seminary studies for astronomy—and that way traded heaven
for the sky; I never took as a lover the famous but stumbledrunk
opera tenor whose name I cannot here divulge, though he
and I like the stars were of the same mold and burning in affinity; and
at night in the observatory we never disported and wondered which

of the glass—the telescope lens leading high or the wine decanter going
increasingly low—could take a man farthest.

My name isn't Patience; I wasn't a stillbirth; I
wasn't even a stillbirth.

My name isn't Hamilton; and I was never 10; I never
gobbled grampa's Ladies Church League First Prize watermelon
entirely on the Fourth of July; and ran to the creek, to wash off; and
ran, I was as slick as a seed, and ran, past the burnt knoll, to the fields
where a mower whipped round at the charge of a wasp and his scythe
neatly severed my windpipe.

My name isn't Maysie; I wasn't released
at age 18 from the orphanage, to be a kerchiefed gypsy phrenologist
traveling with my monkey (Kip) and my body in bangles and taffeta,
a life of coins and kisses I would never trade to be a Queen; and
all the better for seeking out clues of my parentage, here
in a hedgerow, there in the chinese tea, wherever; I didn't find
my mother, a lovely colored woman the shade of a fawn's far underbelly,
of high rank in a Boston philanthropic society
dedicated to aiding her people, she had a room in a house
done up in sheaves of pressed African flowers and Mexican crucifixes,
and had that same excitement in her bones; I didn't find
my father, and who knows how many others' father, I didn't
approach an open window at dusk in that battlemarked slattern
of a house on Mickle Street, no; and if it happened, and
it didn't, I was 36 by then and he was ancient and ageless;
a candle was lit; he was writing; the hat he kept on was a crumpled
gray, the soft and shapeless gray of a dray-nag's muzzle,
his beard was that very color bleached by a shade; but the vase
was a fire of pinks and tiger lilies; he looked up from the page;
he didn't really see me, I could tell his eyes were still filled
with the page; and yet they said to me, *you are my child;* not
that it happened, it didn't; I left; a steady
current of people filled the street, alive and loud; his
eyes might have said it with just as much claim
to a hundred of them, in May, in Camden, New Jersey, in 1885.

And now we have read the books they write about our father,
singing his praises. This is the phrase they use: "singing his praises."

We, who never existed enough in his life, have read the singing
of the praises that never existed enough in his life, and now
from where we abide in the spaces between things touching, we
would like to sing his praises too. An antimatter chorus.
We would like to praise his words, they are so comely
in acceptance of the world with all of its rank perfume that sticks
in the creases and glazes over by morning, his words
that took the speech of horse-car conductors and walkup girls and
gave it the indigo-iridescent louse-ridden cosmos-connoitering
wings it deserves. We praise the ink of his words, it
is blacker and deeper than outer space though it fits in its
6-oz. crystal. And we praise the squid, that king
of all insomnia—whose ink glands mean perpetual night
is a living thing, tucked in its body. That king of diversion,
whose ink is a dummyself hanging credibly sized and shaped
in the waters—guardianangel-, golem-, doppelgänger-ink.
(And wasn't our father's ink his public being?) And
especially we praise the squid of the deep, we mean the *deep*,
where the waters are black and ink would be useless, but its
is a luminous cloud, a waft of bright light, a lamé.
(And wasn't our father's? Yes—wasn't our father's?) Now
a dozen squid are folded over a clothesline while the fishers finish
stacking their gear. We praise their knuckles a day's work's
rubbed dull garnet. We praise the air of the Greek islands over them
and in them, it has more dead than the air of some other places and
more honorable dead (we've seen our father open
Homer; marbled paper should be praised, and the raised
hubs of leatherbound spines). For every death filling the air, the lungs
have one accommodating alveólus, and this is efficient, fitting
synergy and cycling, so we praise the human body, every subatomic
pokerchip in the vast halls of its house rules. We
can never sing praises too many. Of even a rhizome, a protein,
one bulbette of roe. We have been waiting
in the null-spaces, here in the Byways of Possible Combination
one pi-meson wide, and we want to tell you those spaces are nothing
but genesis song. Sing with us. Simply be silent and
hear yourself sing. We are going to praise the almost-nothing
colors of malt and barley, in their barrels next to the dried green peas

and salt cod. We are going to sing for every string of sudden stiffening
below a nipple that flies it like a kite, for every wire
in a radio that's carried the news of murder in alternation
with the lyrics of love (doo-*wah*), for the life of the bottom-quark
(in trillionths of a second) and the life of the tortoise whose shell
time buffs to lustre its emerald burls over generations of men,
we're going to sing these praises and nothing can stop us, please
join in, we're going to sing of the perfect angle the beak of the
bluetit makes in territorial ardor, of the chipped hand
of a satyr on a bisque Pompeian vase, then of the chipped foot
of the maiden posed in flight, and how the signalman who's motioning
a jetliner into its bay is an eloquent stylized da Vinciesque figure
deserving of place in a pottery frieze for future archeological tweezers,
and of the moon, and of the nematode, and of the star-nosed mole,
and of the rumble of the moving van, and of the flash of a knife that
flashes other knives into the glare like one fish flicking
a whole silver school on its axis, and of a single scale in that school
distributing light's Newtonian range, of spare change
jiving in a pocket like an *a cappella* group in a basement club, the notes
they hit, and of the rose, and of the word *rose,*
and of the streetmarket bowl of roses on his writing-table this
otherwise grimed-over day in the late spring on Mickle Street, the book
he's writing, the room around a book or even a single poem
that's through now though the song itself, the cellsong
and the sunspotsong, is never through, and
we will sing the praises of you
and you will sing the praises of us, too.

Radio Pope

Here come the oddballs, the goofballs, all
of the shuffle-gaited in mien or thought,
pariahs scratching their pants up
into their cracks, the slow and equally
the insolently speedy, here they come, the weirdos
and wackos of our own genetic plasmpool,
lolloping with two left feet and four eyes
over their acreage of spilled drinks,
here they stumblingly come,
the shunned, the ones with the black shades drawn
like high schools during air raid drill,
so no stray light will give itself away
no matter how zealously it burns in there,
and it burns in there, by night it burns and by day.

I thought he was fevered, I did, the first time
that I saw it. I was five, and I'd been fevered
with the various speckled ailments of being
three and four and five, and always he'd see me
through these with the mumbled love
and chin-chucks of a clumsy affection I later
learned to think of as a monumental tenderness
some sculptor began in stone but then abandoned.
(Once, I remember, he kissed my cheek pretending
it scalded his lips.) And so I thought: yes, now
he's running a temperature too, *I'll* need
to care for *him*. In minor ways, I cared for him
the next eleven years. Oh but it wasn't a fever; or not
that kind. He'd found another radio.

Some are lustrously umber-and-ebony tortoiseshell
in that 1950s plastic made to be as deep as La Brea
and withstand howitzer practice. Some are set in cabinets
of walnut as finely tooled as the coffins of oil magnates.
"Gemchest" (1928) is a rich metallic blue,
its grill a mythic Chinese waterbird in diecut silhouette,
while "Snapper" (1950) simulates the look of alligatorskin
in crazed black plastic. Some are leathered. Some
are louvered. You need to know the language.
Breadboards. Beehives. Tombstones. Some are elegantly
peaked cathedrals. Some are chorus girls with lightbulb boobs.
"Globetrotter." "Coronet." "Space Ace." "Egyptica."
"Whisperette." "Transitone." "Dutchess." "The Gypsy."
"Rhythm Baby." "Synchrophase-400." "Little Miracle."

He'd found another *radio* . . . *sputter* . . . *crackle* stone
"as Gigantick around as the Head of an Ogre. And I
would very cheerfull deem it a Peruke-stand—but
the Veining at its *temples* and *jaw* is Glittering
to such degree that it needs be commodated
to my Grotto"—Alexander Pope. The year is 1740.
". . . encrusted," says Peter Quennell, "with Cornish diamonds,
branches of coral, lumps of amethyst, crystals and quartzes,
'fossile' specimens, coloured Brazilian pebbles, knobs of ore . . ."
Now Pope is dancing on his bandylegs around this
fresh addition, "as rowzed as by a cowslip wine." And
now he lifts it to his ear, then stills: as if his own
excitements were invasive, and could tease some dreamy
murmur out of the lithic core.

Not to mention the "novelties"—a stations-bearing
schooner-in-a-bottle; a plastic wiener slathered-up
in plastic mustard, and blathering FM jazz or AM news; two
versions of an equestrian Hopalong Cassidy (Topper rearing
in one; one, not); an elf; an elephant; a treasure chest
with gold doubloons for dials . . . His favorite was *so*
plain, though, it resembled a toaster won at bingo,
a silver-sided "Melody-mate" he used to listen to
with her, all lovey-poo, and who-knows-what: I maybe
began as a lull between two 1952 top hits one night.
And what did he *think?*—some mystery pemmican
of a dead wife might be rattling around inside
its snags of tubes and wires, waiting to be moistened back
to life? He collected sixteen of the things.

And Raymond Chase's collection of 1,370 bricks.
"I like bricks and I find bricks fascinating. So I joined a group
of other people who like bricks." They meet twice a year
—the International Brick Collectors Association.
Lovers of the Stinking Rose (for garlicphiles)
has 3100 members. And the Miniature Book Society
(definition: under three inches high). The Werewolf
Research Center has 30 members, who meet annually
at the WolfCon ("This is a dangerous business,"
Executive Director Stephen Kaplan says). And yes,
the Matchbook Society (1500 members; Evelyn Hovious owns
5 million matchbooks). And the sugar packet collectors.
Saddlebags. Fishing lures. Marbles. Sand. (*Sand?* 300 members.)
And yes, the radio clubs. And yes, and yes, the radio clubs.

In Kansas, in August, the sun is a solvent.
The land peels back like cracked leather, and
around its edges a chaffy, yolky promise of gold
billows into the air. I'd sift the fields for arrowheads
(a steer skull once, I lovingly becrayoned) while
he'd deftly finagle the tag price on some yard sale
"Listenmaster" or "Never-Static" ever lower.
All the year, we'd weekend down to every Babel of junk
clumped teeteringly between Blackwell and Waco, but
summers opened up the whole of his Rand-McNally foldouts
into enterable adventure—the Road! the Beckon! and
then the inevitable pulling out of the blazing late-day sky
to sit in dinge, in a den of like-minded folk
displaying their beautiful boxes of ghosts.

Here come the jokers, the jackoffs, the jerks,
the festive wearers of lavishly tasseled fezzes,
here they come, no *more* and no *less*
than the owlishly bespectacled, the labsmocked
and the bibliocentric sent by Fate to weight this otherwise
soapbubble planet in studiousness,
and by their garb, and by their jargon, they know
their own, by nametag and by intricate ritual handshake,
here come Dykes on Bikes and here come Moms Against Bombs,
the clans, the banded-together, and by their squirting
pinky rings and by their prayershawls, similar spirits
hearken and conjoin, and be they rabbis, hey or be they
flingers of cowpies, each seeks mirroring in peerage, don't they now o
reader of poetry, o fellow reader of poetry?

ca-thunk ca-thunk ca-thunk—in Muncie, Walter Berkoff
froggied out his mouth and imitated the sound
of coconut halves doing radio hoofbeats: *imitation*
imitation hoofbeats, wow! I remember so much . . .
In Tuscaloosa. Sheboygan. The floor is linoleum
under "throw rugs." The mood is frivolous but the room is
dim, as if they need to play at being illicit, as if
they need to pass their radios around the room like
samizdat. Conspiratorial. Hunted. One (well, twelve
or so) of a kind. I'd be the only child and, most times,
the only girl in a world of a dozen sweet and
stogie-smokin' men. The singlest thing inside a scene
of singularity, I'd waken on a ledge of seven clunker
radios set in a row. The aroma of fat havanas.

"Some Men, like Pictures, are fitter for a corner
than a full Light . . ." "Solitudinous" in his *Grott,*
amongst "Spars Minerals & Marbles," of course
he came to praise the ways of those
who shared his passion, as well as those who donated it
forms. The Prince of Wales donated six urns.
"A length of Roman ruin from the Reverend Mr. Spence."
"A man not only shews his Taste but Virtue,
in the Choice of such Ornaments . . ." (so) ". . . in this sense,
the Stones may be said to Speak." Red Mundic.
Pieces of the Eruptions from Mount *Vesuvius.*
Brain-stones Snake-stones Blood-stones Flints.
"A fine and very uncommon Petrifaction come from
Okey-hole in *Somersetshire,* from Mr. Bruce."

because the first
                    of anything is
            separation
the knife   at the cord   (or
on another level
                    the Expulsion
        from Eden   one life
                            large)
we meet   we meet
            in assembly
        as if to counteract that
severing
            and the greater
                            one to come

And Cowboys for Christ has 83,000 members.
Even the Brotherhood of Knights of the Black Pudding Tasters
has 2,000. The American Gourd Society: 2500.
The National Clogging and Hoedown Council claims 846.
Of course the American Fancy Rat and Mouse Association
consists of only 150, but quantity isn't the point
here. In Toronto, in 1972, eight people convene
"to attempt to construct a ghost." For over a year,
eight "sitters" weekly meet and concentrate, creating
"Phillip," who raps on tables or sometimes tilts or
even overturns the tables—this, on call and in front
of credible witnesses. "Phenomena produced
do not seem to result from one individual." No, "they
seem to require the presence of at least four of the group."

Some *never* worked. Some gargled dots of megahertz,
but then a pure effluvium of story or song
—the wireless wonder in all of its warmed-up glory—
warbled forth, and these they'd gather around
like druids at oraclestones. Or if one fizzled
in the middle, someone pitched in with a credible rendition
of *The Shadow* or *Amos and Andy* or *Lum and Abner*.
Rico Beazley did an amazing Kate Smith. "You have a good face
for radio," goes an old joke, and he had, it glimmered dully
in their circle like a twelve-pound ball of suet, although
his singing loaned it beauty. And some specialized
in Orson Welles; or FDR's "fireside chats"; or
. . . endless minor passions. City-states of individual need
within the confederacy.

I swear he could spot the sexy hunched-up shoulder
of a deco "Grantline 502" or a "Tune-about" peeking
one inch out of a nine-foot pile of Chevy axles,
castoff baby carriages, and cans of crusted slop.
My eye got sharpened over time too, like a dull gem
polished endlessly at a lapidarist's wheel until it shone.
We had canteens, a compass . . . darlin', we were
mobilized for radio the way another lesser species might be
all paraphernalia'd for sex or bear. By day
we baked like clay in the sun; or raced long clouds
that brushed the tufted horizon like freight trains. And
by night I'd doze asleep beneath the broadcast moon,
the full blank moon where all of the planet's stations
overlap into a perfect white static.

Where does it start? Can we say that it starts
in the pre-Australopithecine dark
of the caves, between any two people who "talk" without seeing?
Does it start in 1865?—Maxwell is developing the theory.
In 1887?—Hertz is sending the first waves. Or Marconi
('*n cheese,* I always thought as a child)?—that's 1899.
But let's say it's 1912 right now and a young man,
David Sarnoff, in a room on Nantucket Island where he works
relaying messages for American Marconi, receives
the impossible news of the White Star liner Titanic. Later:
I have in mind a plan of development which would make radio
a household utility, in the same sense as a piano or a phonograph . . .
What is it about the first stated burst of a vision that makes us shiver?
. . . the receiver can be designed in the form of a "radio music box" . . .

We were in a diner, sinking our fleet of oyster crackers into the chili,
when he rushed out: two humongous shitkick dogfaced types
were pitching radios out of our back seat into their flatbed.
First he just watched, stunned. But at the tenth he ran
straight at them like a pebble slingshot into a wall. A tooth
was gone and an ear torn by the time I hustled over—I was
eight—and stood in front of him and crossed my arms and told them
"That's my daddy." They stopped. They goggled. They could have
mushed us both, but laughed instead, dusted him off, and marched
us into the diner, treating us royally to apple pie and malts.
A year later, I came home early from school: he was in bed
with a lady, a stranger. "Scramola," he told me. I was hurt; but
it helped, remembering: the vital tenth of those radios, that so
shook him, was a "Melody-mate," one of the ones where my mother's
   ghost lived.

Here come the skinheads, the deadheads, everyone
swastika'd and flaming skull'd and all-cap tattooed
FUCK SLUTS or possibly DUKES OF SCUM
by razorblade and dimestore ink; their breath stinks
like their boot toes; and their boot toes, like
the blood running out of your ass. Here come the saints,
the pained-and-sunken-cheeked-but-shining,
in their aureoles like fingerprints
left by the late-at-night touch of the Lord Almighty;
solo in their suffering, the saints go marching in,
at last, in a cluster like fresh white bottles of milk.
Here come the Wobblies, the Mugwumps, the Commies,
the lobbyists, the DAR Grand Matron in her silver rinse,
the Kleagle in his eye-holed sheet—preaching at the minions.

Once or twice he slapped me—*hard*. But I was
half-hellacious hundreds of times; and so I figure that more
than evened out. "Sheesh. *You're* a doozie," he'd tell me
after, rubbing cool Noxzema into the sting. They always ask me
now, do I regret my "wayward" childhood? I'll tell you
this: it got damn claustrophobic at those meetings, like being
inside the clammy hold of a body cavity, when suddenly
all of its dental fillings picked up morning farm reports or swing.
A little idiotic, a little . . . "wayward," okay, sure. But I'll say
this, too: I was nine in 1957, I spent my time around
their simple, driven love; and in a nation readying
for serial assassination, breaking of the public trust, and endless
bouts of indignity, rancor, and pigjaw greed, I witnessed
this innocence flowering too, with malice toward none, in the corners.

"The Ostrych will swallow & then Regurg. his Stone
—Obtain one? Also today a handbill—that a *lithophagus*
Soamey Williams will swallow Iron & Flints; & Stones
the smallest of it being the size of a Pigeons Egg, and
in his Stomack you may hear them rattle as if in a Sack"
and then, of course, "—Obtain one?" Pope,
in a letter. Pope, and his network of curiosa fanciers,
gardeners, archeology esotericists. Toad-stones.
Brindle-stones. Stones from a *(Spewed)* Volcanoe.
Shark-stones. An alabaster Pan. A Gem, I hear it
is from a bird made All of Gems. "Obtain one." Yes,
and in the Old Myths, weren't there stones that talked,
that transmuted metal,
that knew things? Orient coins. Saints' ash. Whyte coal.

Not to mention the ancillary ephemera of every stripe,
like yellowing copies of *Radio News* and *Radio Digest;*
manufacturers' catalogues; a Melvin Purvis
Secret Service Agent Scarab Ring in its chintzy shimmer . . .
Such small scraps, for such large longing! In
Des Moines, on my eleventh birthday (I remember:
Ray and Jeri Wexler had frosted and candled a gutted
"Super Sound"), Dick Ortle treated us (once
again) to his sincere rendition of Veronica
"Big Band" Donahue's "Sorry Blues" as three big
trucker-looking collectors wept, at that voice
as clear as a 13th-century highlands stream. I cried too, not
at the beauty so much, but at how *important* it was
to him, out of all the world. Now *that* was sad.

They concentrate; the air gets densed; then . . . *rap /* and
rap / and "Phillip" "exists" or doesn't "exist," depending
on your philosophic stance and if you aren't sure,
the GRS (Ghost Research Society) *is* (or isn't, but isn't
with an openness) as well as the Society
for the Systematic Documentation of Paranormal Experiments,
the Psychic Science International Special Interest Group,
the MetaScience Foundation, the Psychic Detective Bureau,
or PROTEUS (Project to Research Objects,
Theories, Extraterrestrials and Unusual Sightings), all
of which are concentrating, as much as the accordion collectors
and aficionados of windmills or thimbles or striptease are,
and the air gets densed with group will, and whatever "is"
or "isn't" out there, rouses itself, and responds.

"Lissome": did I say that I was "lissome"? I was
butter—I was butter *on fire*—desiring being "lissome,"
a term I'd read in the pages of *Radio Romance*. There was a boy
in Fort Smith, Arkansas, whose wiffled grin and man's hands
made my skin leap up like a crowd in a burning theater,
though the crowd didn't *want* to leave—it *liked* this burning,
oh very much. *That* was a month! That was a gala month
in the milo at night—and then I was on the road again with The Radio
   Pope
my Dad, and my love my true love was a blue electron
spinning in our rearview mirror. I *raged*. On my eleventh
birthday fat Dick Ortle sang "Sorry Blues."
On my fifteenth birthday Dick Ortle was *still* singing
"Sorry Blues." They were dedicated to sameness,
and I wasn't the same. I was "lissome" and "lorn."

X happened; Y happened; then, incredibly,
C happened!—all of it, done, and gone, and completely
sacrosanct from the besmirchy touch of the present.
In fact, the past is perfect. Roughly lived
until it's a tatter stinking with use, the past is still
the paradigmatic virgin. We turn our faces its way
with ten thousand forms of amazement. Now a man
is reading a scholarly work on Alexander Pope
(200 years ago—more!) who's in his garden fondly contemplating
his antique urns and statuary relics
—perfect. Even ruined, they're perfect. He fusses
with their placement, cants his wig at a rakish angle,
whistles, fusses, fusses, whistles. Ah—especially
ruined and forever ruined—perfect!

"Jeepers creepers." "Geez Louise." In a long-outmoded
Magnavox model, somebody's saying "banana oil" or "daddy-o,"
and blowing rings from a Chesterfield, driving a new DeSoto.
The brio of uniformed Western Union boys
on their zip-by bikes. The *shish* of pinochle dealed.
Sousaphones. Brogans. Stove-heated curling irons.
This radio is a crate, is a shipment
of diner counter mustard pots (with those small wooden oars
to trowel it thick, and a notch in the lid for the oar).
A porkpie hat. A watch-and-fob. Resort marimba music
punctuates the darkness over the moonlit lake.
It's anytime, it's once-upon-a-time. "Bunk,
brother—don't feed me that hooey!" And later:
"Not there. *There*."—in a softer voice.

This happened in Terre Haute, on August 16. I was
sixteen too. It happened at a Midwest Old-Time
Radio Collectors Jamboree at Norm and Deedee's house.
Their son-in-law was home and drunk and followed me
out to the car and pushed me down to the gravel and
bunched my skirt up over my waist and punched me
bad, in the belly. I'd been carrying a rare vacuum tube
that shattered, and I raked its jagged glass edge
over his face, and ran. I was safe back in the house.
And where had my father been, my Paladin Daddy who *I*
protected dozens of times? I found him in the basement
slumped like a rag doll over a "Melody-mate," and
never to collect another shred again, in this world.
       I sold each of the stinking radios.

This is, I think, a fine, a *salient,* place at which to leave him:
Pope is in receipt of a bucketful of *petrifacted ferns,*
they look like molds for the making of faery ladders.
Every spore-hung rung of them, miraculously detailed!
They arrived as a happy gratuity with a linen-wrapped basket
of Jersey shells, a gift from Aaron Hill, and this
confluence of affinities is—as much as the sought-for
specimens themselves—a good reason *the Rhapsode rises up*
in my Pip-squeak Carcase today and crows! Lord Bathurst,
Baron William Digby, Martha Blount . . . his weave
of kindred spirits, ever tighter, ever more fantastickall. Yes, this
is a fitting place to leave him, jigging with meticulous steps
around the bucket, composing a letter of thanks in his head
. . . *which I have found most grottofying* . . .

The Bauergoths from Kokomo showed up, and
Eddie "Transistor" Frink, and Tito Stein who
cracked his knuckles annoyingly during the sermon part.
Me?—I was calm, and catered-to, and didn't need
convincing by the pastor's sappy parables: my whole life
I'd been taught that the juices of human existence
swim the air as wavelengths, so if *that's* what he intended
I was preconvinced. And I was busy imagining a future
of floral kitchen curtains and boys. Goodbye
to the highway! Goodbye to the back rooms stacked with trash!
I lived with cousins then, but that's another story. There
were many stories, many boys, and many nights with them, and more
than once a dream: something, I don't know what, but something
is left behind on a highway and I'm frantic at the loss.

The stars: incendiary. The stars: far back in time.
Our lives on earth: a matter of heavy daily plodding.
Our loves: a matter of daily plodding. Sometimes
our loves: incendiary. The stars: a fire
sent through time. Our dreams: a matter of earth
and a matter of stars, in mixture. Our loves:
as if propelled by burning dreams far back in time.
The stars: a fire sent through time, and turned to language
on earth, by radiotelescopes. Our lives on earth:
receivers. The stars: transmission devices. The burning: a message
carried through our heavy daily plodding. I imagine
two people wake, in the caves. They can't see
one another. They "talk": the stars,
the dreams, the dailiness, the love. And it begins there.

To: M
From: Sam
Re: Your positioning A.a.
  Truly—*Australopithecus afarensis* is
simply your best work yet! They look
as if they might grumble, and snap off some
unwary 10-year-old's finger at any moment.
T. says choosing an arm-linked male and female
gives an impression of nuclear family pairing
unsubstantiated blah blah by the fossil record but he's
a dried up fuck of a fossil himself, and speaking
of pairing: I'm arriving at the symposium
by 5 o'clock, and bringing hunger for dinner and you.

I delivered a powerhouse paper at the colloquium
in Rome, if over two hundred requests for offprints are a gauge
(and, later, an NEH grant) though the first loose wave
of applause was as thrilling as anything. Let me explain:
my work is constructing museum diorama models
figurated as accurately as possible from paleontology
evidence. For prehistoric reconstruction, interpretation
is necessary (were there eyebrows? no one knows) and
wearying. The work is lonely. Accuracy (say, capillaries
in eyeballs) is exacting. Twice a year we meet, for papers
and for parties. Internationally belaureled dioramacists
jet in from every major scholarly nook on the globe. We call ourselves
The Institute; by what frayed thread are we kept
from being one of my father's radio clubs?

d found another radi

          time is entropy

      fields for arrowhea   is

breakage

      alabaster Pan   is

    recombina

marimba   *sputter*

   crazy   frag

     crackle

ments get through

     "Sorry Bl

the receiver can be designed in the form of

  hunger for   *utter*

      radio

I'm not saying this really happened.
It happened, though. I was alone
in the lab. You have to understand: I was surrounded
by faces hanging from the beams like wheels of cheese
in a dim-lit European grocery. Grabby Sam
who *is* a dear had made me a gift of a human skull
I'd set as appropriate decoration on my desk, and
in a weird and idle mood I started doodling on it,
coloring it—with crayons, you know? . . . and then everything
flooded me, *everything,* the fields, the meetings, the smell
of the Buick's upholstery, and a voice streamed out of the skull.
My father's voice I hadn't heard for sixteen years. And
it was blurred, but if I concentrated, I could tune it
clearer. *Lost it* . . . (concentrating) . . . *Here it comes* . . .

Here come the covens,
the enclaves, congregations, unions,
packs, gangs, rallies and leagues,
the amalgamated thises-and-thatses,
those who measure their cohesiveness in angstroms,
those who reckon it by the thundering trumps of the seraphs themselves,
here come the amassed abused, here come the schools
of their tormentors, here come the encongressed
and societal, the loyal orders, the camps and committees
of every displayable suasion, both the bug-eyed and the blind,
here come Aladdin Knights of the Mystic Light
(1,000 listed), "dealers, collectors and users" (it *says*
"users") "of Aladdin lamps" as if enough might
rub, and wish, and so quicken the cold and lifeless.

It only happened that once. I'm not insisting
you believe me. Everything quieted. He said my name.
He said my mother's name. He said,
in intermittent stretches of reception clarity, many things
and most of them cliché—*It doesn't stop, it thins
but it doesn't stop,* I remember. (Is this
what I *wanted* to hear, so heard?) It doesn't stop,
although it doesn't exactly continue: it's more
like a joining. He told me the hell with the pouters and naysayers,
go ahead, love it up, tussle it, rumple its skin
while you've *got* it! That's what he said, in a voice like a powder.
He said he was waiting—not "him," not "waiting," exactly. More
like a joining—an organization, a worldwide organization, and
one day I'd join it too, he said. There wasn't any rush though.

Meet and rejoin me, in the pensive Grott

—POPE

The Importance of Artists' Biographies

was soon so great that the enduring fame of several [early]
Greek artists—Zeuxis and Apelles, to name but two—rests
on these biographies alone, without there having been any
possibility of later forming an impression of their actual works.
—ERNST KRIS AND OTTO KURZ

The days go by, then more days go by.
We've all seen a lover from fifty feet, and walked up
to a stranger. Though the stars at fifty
light years are clear. The nights go by,
then more nights go by. We've all leapt on
and in a lover, then fifty minutes later rolled
off a stranger. The air goes farther than eyes go
through it, the days and nights are small
collections on a desktop—matchbooks,
knuckle-sized shells, these opened pages of Kris and Kurz—,
a space takes place
between a life and the attributes of a life,
we've all seen it.

✶ ✶ ✶

Dürer once painted a spider over
a picture by Michelangelo. And a
good few lucid-looking lovers
of art were duped—the threshold having
been lowered between a life and a credible fiction of life,
by a rod, one causative cone, enough
for an otherwise-discerning aficionado to be going
down the gallery in her floorsweeping silks, her hands
on every picture as if they were fruits to be tested,
as if she does this all of the time and with any drawing,
as if, in a crowd of men from the court,

before Michelangelo's gilt-framed sketch she
hadn't especially tried to squash it.

———

And—if Dürer had wholly webbed over
that surface—webbed it to opacity—then
would we know

———

by the broke-nosed, doleful face; the
father's entreaties to turn away from marble, mallets,
mixing-plaques, and the drafty shambles-strewn room;
the nights the Prior allowed him in
with a candle and chalk, to let the flame lick
intermittently up
the legs, the groins, the chest skin now thin as shellac
on the corpses of San Spirito, getting it
down exact; the story of the faked
Sleeping Cupid; the story of the blows with the Pope;
the "great distress of mind and fatigue . . . better
if I had set myself to a cartwright!"; the sonnets,
concerned with absolute beauty opening
like a flower, and the fifteen-year-old boys
he saw as flowers; that, all that, and more, or
just the way the gray veins in his hands' backs
bulged, the only indication of terrible weight, as he rested
his head in the sunstruck floury dust
of the studio, with a mother's gesture of setting her only
child into bed—then

———

would we know to know
the swaths of cloud-borne-glow and
galactic deepnesses, the artisan-like
concentration and bunch-muscled effort of God,
in Michelangelo's charcoal rough
for *Division of Light from Darkness* . . .
would we?

✦ ✦ ✦

Later, in a garden, the courtiers gone back
to the massive halls of power, she'll look at a
real spider doing the business of spiders
among some stems, and idly wonder: what

———

it must have been, to be the first man—or
maybe she'll think it as woman—to see, to really see,
this creature as itself: a black-backed
stalk-eyed sac-bellied pinch-jawed scuttler on too
many too bristled legs. *And would I know,
from that, the nubbin inside
that lets out length after length of this delicate
engineering, this stuff
a bug-gland's-weight away from being pure
filamented sun . . .*

———

She may not be a lady of the court
come from parrots and cakes, but
my lover
I lifted, I differed away
from any ready semblance, then set down

———

here, on a page, in my study. I recognize
her, though. And you might too if you knew her.
Up in a corner, a spider's spinning this
real web that enters your world
as a word, "web," on a page, "this" page, then
light through a window
lifts the spider as light lifts everything
seeable and brings it, at the same speed
it was just now brought to my eyes,
to the stars.

✦ ✦ ✦

Science fiction is full of these distances.
Quasar travel. Planet hops.
As if a time warp were stranger than time.

The days go by, then more days go by.
Often the world is hollow; a central, a generating,
civilization lives in the shell. These books surmise
its whip wars with The Lizard Tribe and The Worm,
its celestial ballet when the wings are in season,
the sprigs above its parturition doors, its blood dance,
even the simple distilling of lavender and citron
out of the air at night, by the shore of its inner sea . . .
surmise all this by looking at life
as we know it, our own long neighborhood blocks,
the secrets in laundromats' spins and urgent impressions
on notepads left by the phone—as if a man
could walk this city we live in, stop still at the corner of
Zeuxis and Apelles, think deep, and put some law
of inference to work. For him, the Earth might be a
kind of conceptual crystal, and what we call our
autobiographies would only be refractions of some
original light at the core. We've all had the feeling
he's right. The nights go by, then more nights go by.
We've all seen the faces of lovers in sleep
go somewhere, maybe back to their source, and we
lay by the breathing of strangers. We've all seen
the faces return. I couldn't guess the distance between
a word I write and your reception of it, astronomy
hasn't such measure. But everybody's walked
above the bones of the mothers, the bones of the fathers,
the grandparent bones going back to the magma
heart of it all, through dragon bones, the flightbones
of a pegasus, the first fine organization of grains
of bone in a luminous nucleus . . . There are spaces
so vast, words fail, light fails, though maybe the crossing
is only from a day to another day.

✷ ✷ ✷

And if the blue look that came over Zeuxis
after one rough *kylix* too many of that white wine
he washed down the mussels with

                                    meant his
taking the spiral frieze off
that last *kylix,* as the model for his own gold
opulent coruscations of fruit trees
                              we'll
never know, will we, we'll never really know.

———————

In my study, I come close. There's a print
by Saul Steinberg: a desk, and the objects of its
arrangement: a ruler, a spool of gray thread,
a box of matches, an austere shell with only
the slightest blush of vulva-pink inside it,
a sketchbook opened casually to a nuthatch
done from a pencil's bold strokes, the pencil . . .

———————

I take off my glasses, stare at that wall,
I come as close as I can. The desktop
fades to almost never having been.

———————

And out of the blurred hints left, I see
as I've seen up there impossibly for years:
an old man on an old burro,
heading heavily toward the right margin.
For years now, heading away
in their own shape, from the shapes of Steinberg's
placing.
            It's raining. The old man is
violet, and soft—the kinds of small shadows
worn flannel casts. The burro is weary. It isn't
giving up, though. They're carrying something
—the small tools of a life. Perhaps he's a peddler,
and this is his work, that comes out of
the work of others.

A spider remains in a corner through all of this,
a lover remains in my bed. The night,

the sightless webbed-over night, goes by,
then it's day. It happens that way.
The sketchbook in my Steinberg print is fixed
to a page marked "nuthatch," fixed unturnably,
though it's day, then it's night, and in a way
time turns that world as I can turn pages
in Kris and Kurz . . .
                              An asterisk calls
attention elsewhere. So this is the shape
of a spider, that I've taken off a "real" wall
for this "wall," on this page. It's morning.
A lady I know is still asleep. Light lifts a spider.
Light lifts the lady, and lifts me, though I never move,
and light lifts a spider. The birth of our sun
is first being seen on other planets, a flash
some registerial hand beyond
our understanding duly records. A spider is one
continuous tunnel of being a spider, as long
as light is long, as far; and if the cosmos
curves, a spider returns, at least
a picture of spider returns—as we return, merely
by the saying of that, to Dürer. For him,
it's another morning. He adds one last
perfectionist's dab to the little wiseass joke he's played
in a square inch of Michelangelo. He looks up
now, confused for a moment, confused and exalted,
as if . . . There are times when we're sensitized to it . . .
The whole air around him is pictures,
the light is a gallery. Nothing, he sees, can be lost.

DUAL

an essay-poem

The Wheel

I don't believe he did anything indifferently. That formulaic paint-by-number "winter woodland" scene, from my father's attempts to fill his retirement time, is no exception: every empty cusp and ganglion was filled to its perimeters exactly, as if a slip of his fussing brush might cause a similar slip in gravity or the seasons. I can see him double-checking, that the tube of black in his hand was also "8," to match the number in some tiny blank arena— holding the tube to the living-room light, as if appraising the soul inside it.

They were all "black," "green," "white," "red," as I remember; there weren't dubious mixes, "salmon" or "rhubarb" or "gunmetal blue." And of course their borders never overlapped, an idea like "scumbling" was another universe's altogether. No, each flat patch held itself intact and separate, like the tiles of a mosaic or the coexistent shapes of a stained-glass window inside their leadings.

Still, the effect was uncanny: step back just enough, and the eye comprised them into a single seamless stretch of snowed-over landscape. It had depth, it could be entered.

When I walk there now, when I idly kick its fresh dry snow into quick white wings, or trace the serial commas of ice along a branch's belly, when I'm *in* it, I can see that no thing's one thing. Ice is water. The shadow that's gray is also lavender. My own face is and isn't my father's. Simple truths.

In twilight—twin light—anything can happen. One day, a bird—a winter bird, as edged as scrap metal—leisurely hung in that pallid winter sky. It was moving, of course, but distance gave it the look of a single black flaw in those turbidly milky heavens. And then it divided: two birds. They must have been mating. I thought of the story of Jacob, the moment his psyche divides the angel-part out of the man.

At Tabby Katt's Exotic Dancers, the women say one thing only, the way we *all* do, at our jobs. I guess I'm supposed to say "the humanities." What *they* say, in the terms of my father's regiment of tubes, is decidedly "scarlet." They're one supple muscle of sexual beckon, often coy in the first song; by the third, spread open like butterflied shrimp. I've seen sad clubs like this, but in the happy ones the dancers and their audience share a great raw camaraderie, and the money is good, a green river. People are pleased to pay, to be shouted that one scarlet thing.

And yet you know with another part of your brain—some of these women are mothers, and the five-year-old is mysteriously stippled with a painful rash; they're daughters, and somebody's father is signing the bankruptcy papers, somebody's father is shyly accepting the Engineer of the Year award; they're biker mamas and novice political activists and budding artists: somebody's wondering vaguely if the foreplane jade-and-amaranth swatch is dry yet . . . Chantilly is also Elizabeth; Candy is also Maude.

Last August, Lady J, the manager, upgraded to a row of flashing strobes; a snazzy haze effect from a nozzle that sprays out talcum; and The Wheel, the size of a dashboard wheel but set in the ceiling over the stage, with which the dancers dizzyingly spin themselves into perfect columns of lickerish skin. When Neely uses The Wheel, she whirls so centrifugally fast, so long, I wonder if her blood is going to separate its cells, red, white. Or maybe she'll suddenly *stop!*—and both of her selves will be standing there, next to each other.

No Distinctions

There are no pews or benches yet; the prayerful bring cushions, or sit in the straw on the floor. It's draughty. You're seated next to someone disfigured badly by disease, whose skin is like a damp gray omelette. Ah, but when the choir beatifically gaggles in; and invisible, aural vaults of Gregorian chant are architected antiphonally in the air, complex yet lightsome; and the village's pride, its vaguely pomegranate-shaped censer, releases its billowy wafts . . . then a man or a woman can also be ascendatory, and rise in fumes, in a radiant plumage of fumes, to the foot of the throne of Heaven.

Our workaday world of salt in the eyes, and death in ambush around any corner, and voices whispering out of the empty dusk, of impossibly painful Solomonic choices that need declaring—this world is filled with mysteries. Surely the Church elucidates some of the murk: such-and-such is the one true path, while this-and-that is not. But when you enter the Church in an uplands British village in the year 1250—or anywhere, really; anytime—the mysteries you leave in the shadowy entrance hall, you simply trade for Mysteries, the Big Ones, including the twofold nature of Jesus the Christ.

For Jesus is the Son of the Lord God: "Lo, a voice from Heaven did say 'This is my beloved Son, in whom I am well pleased.'" But Jesus is also the "Son of man"—six times, this appellation is scattered throughout the New Testament, there, I suppose, at least in part as a reminder of the essentially *homo sapiens* hurt and sinfulness and grandeur he shares or seemingly shares with the rest of us. Born of the seed of the Holy Spirit, from out of the rended smatters of mortal flesh, "I am Alpha," he says, "and Omega." We like this cosmic paradox, the encompass, in a Messiah.

We like it far less glimpsed amid the congregation. Here, the combination of opposite attributes bespeaks a horrible chaos. Mary Douglas says, "It is only by exaggerating the difference"—not embodying it—"between within and without, above and below, male and female, with and against, that a semblance of order is created.

"For example, when a monstrous birth occurs, the defining lines between humans and animals may be threatened. If a monstrous birth can be labelled an event of a peculiar kind the categories can be restored. So the Nuer treat monstrous births as baby hippopotamuses, accidentally born to humans and, with this labelling, the appropriate action is clear. They gently lay them in the river where they belong."

The religious lore of the world is rich in hermaphrodite deities (Jesus is often depicted with a pronunciation of "feminine" features). Mircea Eliade: "The ambivalence of the divinity is a constant theme to the whole religious history of humanity," and "the hermaphrodite (as a god) represented in antiquity an ideal condition which men endeavored to achieve spiritually; but if a child showed at birth any signs of hermaphroditism, it was killed by its own parents."

Much of the punch of Diane Arbus's photograph of "Alberto/Alberta" comes from the fact that it *isn't* hoked up, it's an "everyday" portrait of somebody staring frankly at the camera. "Diane's deceptively simple approach leveled all of her subjects, and made both 'freak' and 'normal,' 'eccentric' and 'middle-class,' appear in some aspects the same. Diane made no distinctions." She'd do a mother-and-child sitting that was as sweetly composed as anyone's, but the mother was stripper Heaven Lee, agleam in titty sequins.

At a museum showing, visitors spit on her photographs.

It is only by exaggerating the difference . . . But Arbus, snapping away in her flophouse, peepshow, loonybin swirl, incorporates: ". . . once they began talking to each other and she started clicking her camera, the gulfs that divided them—gulfs of race, age, expectation, craziness even—momentarily disappeared."

The incense smokily rises, aromatic, disembodied, a perfect symbol of transcendence. We don't want to be reminded it exists as much to mask the stink of packed-in, unwashed bodies, our bodies, our frail, empowered, aging, haunted, tumultuous human bodies, in the year 1250; or anytime.

Parallel Lines

This is what I remember: the light was *so* clear, everything seemed to be bordered as certainly as the black-line drawings in coloring books. My comprehension would "color"—would complete—the world. Each rumple in the sleeves on my jacket cast the shadows of foothills. Each elm leaf shimmered with the individual presence of a garden spade. Where my father's jaw was stubbled it was the neat gray of a helmet strap, and then the pink and sweetly susceptible cheek rose out of that.

Where were we going? I couldn't have yet been five. To Sunday School? He'd walk me there, through the avenues of a Chicago I still thought of—because of his guardedness, and my mother's—as intrinsically clement. Did Sunday School begin before I was five? Is my sister Livia born yet? Nothing's as exact as that light, that pours undeniably over each of its creatures.

A neighborhood "doggie" scampers into our path, and I make a move to go pet it; even as I do, he yanks me back by the jacket cuff, and "doggie" leaps, oblivious to our drama, through a porch's crawlspace lathes. He looks down astonished at me. "Albie," he says (as if they'd ever explained it, as if I'd forgotten a lesson) "that was" (I still recall his voice's violent switch in tenor here, as it fills with the ancient loathing) "a rat."

And later I'd find those optical illusions, where a box is facing into the page, then out, or where a chalice becomes two people's faces in profile. Men who stopped their cars and offered you chocolate were evil. The very light exploded one day, in a gallon jar of layered cherries and sugar my father fermented in the sun for *vishnik,* syrupy home-made brandy, and they let me lick that thickness off the wall, a taste like candy and yet prohibitively adult.

In Hebrew Sunday School, the God that they taught us was fatherly; and "fatherly"—for this was 1953 or -4—became a TV sitcom head-of-household, wise and kind and wearing a tobacco-brown cardigan sweater. In a photograph there are seven of us, in a happy scatter of portable chairs, absorbed in cutting HANUKAH GREE ("tings" yet to come) from construction paper. A God a boy could confide in.

But He also smote the enemy host. He was jealous, and said so, and stored up petty grudges in the cupboards of Heaven, and showed His self on Earth as a menacing fire.

Says Eliade: "What is holy attracts man and at the same time frightens him. The gods reveal themselves as at once benevolent and terrible. In India, beside his gracious and kindly form, each god has a 'terrible form' (*krodha murti*): his fierce and frightening aspect. One of the most frequent Vedic prayers is to be 'delivered from Varuna.' And yet the worshipper cries 'When shall I at last be with Varuna?'"

Jung chronicles the history of "the Christian reformation of the Jewish concept of the Deity: the morally ambiguous Yahweh became an exclusively good God, while everything evil was united in the devil. In the East"—and in my pingpong, back/forth Sunday School understanding—"the gods (Kali is a case in point) could retain their original paradoxical morality undisturbed."

What *were* we to feel, when Abraham meekly obeyed His orders, lifting the blade above Isaac's yielded chickenbone breast? Rembrandt has placed the free hand covering Isaac's upthrust face—at once it bares and tautens the throat; it presses down with awful patriarchal history; it obliterates identity completely, like an ether mask, an ether mask in the shape of some spiderly sea creature, already halfway blotting the bound boy into eternity. The stiff, nay-saying angel in its treacley light can't counterweight this horror.

And what did this have to do with that other father?—Irving Goldbarth, harmless man who tweezed the splinter out of my finger, and checked the fluent working of the tiny bellows of breath in my chest a dozen times during the night, who waited up, who balanced the books, who gently steadied the scared tush for the doctor's shot, who helped the volunteers search for miners' corpses but who openly wept when an adamant thirteen-year-old refused—and I remember: unnecessarily snidely refused—to take part in the Passover *seder*.

Later, JFK was assassinated, "by a lone gunman." Later still, a group of gunmen. Nothing is one thing. No one is one face. Most of my years in graduate school were defined by a series of Nixon's lies. I remembered the dog in his "Checkers speech," and one time I began a (very bad) poem: "I smell a rat here."

I was also lied to in graduate school by a woman whose understanding of the *oeuvre* of Fra Angelico left me breathless, and whose lean and needy body in its slipwork of sexual sweat left me—well, out of breath; two very different, if similar, things. I also lied to her, of course. It wasn't meant meanly; but, convinced that she could never care either spiritually or hormonally for me, I created another me, a *doppel*-me, for her (as it turned out, momentary) delight. The things we do to each other. I've found my notes for another poem from those years, and the quickly-scribbled title is misspelled with an *e* instead of *a:* "Duel."

When Neely's finished her final spotlit split, I buy her a house drink. She's a pleasant few handfuls of spandex, and knows it, and shrewdly plies that knowledge. And in any case, I love to hear their stories. By drink three, I'm getting a smoky-throated earload: when the white-and-black bitch teamup robbed her working clothes in Phoenix; her little sister's hysterectomy; her boyfriend the jazz pianoman, the bastard; she knows CPR; she's seven credits away from an accounting degree. Some giggles, many *looks.* A spectral army of Other People's Neelies gathering around us. Her turn eventually comes up again on the rotation board and she leaves the table, slurring over her shoulder (a joke I think, she's so young after all, but you never *know*), "I was a man before. I had The Operation."

That night, I study my face in the bathroom mirror, looking for traces—how much of Irving Goldbarth adheres, after all of these years, to the boneworks? Fannie Goldbarth—where is she in here? *Exotic ancers* the sign had said, the *d* fallen off, but I don't think there's an "ancer" for these after-midnight solipsistic questions of mine in the oleo-yellow fluorescent light of our bathroom.

Skyler's sleeping; I kiss her even so. I love my wife (it's too simple to think three drinks at Tabby Katt's mean anything else) and a fancy of mine, and always made more powerful when we're beside each other in bed, is that we're parallel lines—we're traveling, at two different speeds, toward the vanishing point, whatever it is, wherever it waits for us Out There.

"Oh Mr. Beer Breath . . ." When I wake, we're each rolled into our separate sides of the sheet, and I think of an opened Torah: its individual, scrolled-up halves; but also the column of revealed text for the day, that they share in common.

A Beautiful Photograph

In a Guggenheim proposal, describing her photographs' subjects, she said, "I want to gather them like somebody's grandmother putting up preserves because they will have been so beautiful . . ."

Preserves . . . / It floats in a jar.

Or: *they* float in a jar—back to back, like spat-defeated lovers feigning sleep, the fetuses contour just enough of their occluded formaldehyde light. We can see their fleshy ridge of connection. We can see their swollen, sausage-casing shapes.

They don't really "float," that's how we're trained to see and say it. They have enormous weight, in part because this grainy half-formed humanness is centered by Arbus in otherwise vacant, otherwise featureless, slapdash sideshow tenting. The one on top faces up, into three or four inches of liquid. The other is bearing it, having its own face softly, dreamily smashed to the bottom glass.

And if, instead, they'd lived? . . . I'm looking now at her famous portrait of the identical twins from Roselle, New Jersey—sisters, maybe six years old. Their matching corduroy dresses are dark; and, standing so symmetrically close that their inner arms overlap, they look as essentially seamed as the fetuses. One is almost pouting. One is almost smiling. Each is almost the other. "Everyone suffers from the limitation of being only one person," she said.

"She would photograph actress Estelle Parsons's twin daughters over and over again; she would photograph elderly twins and twins married to twins . . ."

And of her brother: "It was as if they had passed through some secret experience together . . . they sat or stood, not looking at each other, but close as twins."

And of her husband: "They had the same mournful, watchful expression in their round, dark eyes. Sharing secrets, forbidden pleasures, little indulgences, they had lived like twins so long; it had been their way of surviving."

And of her daughter: ". . . almost identical haunted moonfaces. A private subliminal knowledge seemed to flow between them . . . each was the other's mirror image—the other's twin."

On that deserted stage, in light so tactile it's almost aqueous, grittily aqueous, Arbus's spine-fused fetuses are, like many of her signature works, ethereal and creepy at once. This even could be a diagram of the Creation, as the *Beréshit rabba,* out of the Jewish *midráshim* tradition, tells it: "Adam and Eve were made back to back, joined at the shoulders; then God divided them with an axe stroke, cutting them in two." Eliade: "By the fact that the human race descends from Adam, spiritual perfection consists precisely in rediscovering within oneself this androgynous nature." Plato claims this also explains our lust: the halves' desire to reunite in the shape of the Primal Being.

"I've never heard anyone talk as frankly about sex as Diane Arbus did. She told me she'd never turned down any man who asked her to bed."

"She told how she had followed a dumpy middle-aged couple to their staid East Side apartment. She had sex with both of them, she said. When she maintained she'd had sex with a dwarf or a couple of nudists, her friends would listen—some in awe that she had the courage to go so totally with her obsessions."

The twins are everywhere; or couples on a ballroom floor, the energy of a twirl having blended their bodies; or couples made similar by the creases of age; or the untested smoothness of youth. "Two girls in matching bathing suits, Coney Island, 1967." "The King and Queen of a Senior Citizens Dance, New York, 1970."

And her gallery of those whose twin is inside themselves, an Other under the surface, rising gracefully or tormentedly up—the drag queens, leather lesbians, and half/half carnival freaks of her darkly A.M. forays (laden with her clanking lei of cameras) into what she called "the pits of hell." And she said: "But there's some sense in which I always identify with them."

She said: "A whore I once knew showed me a photo album of Instamatic color pictures she'd taken of guys she picked up. I don't mean kissing ones. Just guys sitting on beds in motel rooms. I remember one of a man in a bra. He was just a man, the most ordinary, milktoast sort of man, and he had just tried on a bra. Like anybody would try on a bra, like anybody would try on what the other person had that he didn't have. It was heartbreaking. It was really a beautiful photograph."

The butch and the fey, the knifed-up and the stripped-down.

"I want to gather them like somebody's grandmother putting up preserves because they will have been so beautiful. I want to save these things, for what is ceremonious and curious and commonplace will be legendary."

Here by Its Absence

The cave art in the Argentines includes—along with those elegant light-footed llama-like beasts of the Ice Age pampas—two hands done in cinnabar on the pale cave wall: one, meatily here by imprinting the color directly from the hand to the rock; the other, having color blown around it through a tube, is here by its absence.

Intermittently, all day, I've seen my father's face. It surfaces in the skins of the faces of strangers, ripples, and vanishes, leaving them jowly or planar or wheaten-cheeked, whatever: like a *déjà vu,* in which a moment is suddenly another moment, as markedly as if steel strutwork shaped it; though—a blink, and it's smoke.

Today nothing is safe from merging into its elseness. Remember the flicker badges they'd sometimes include in cereal boxes?—Batman and his secret identity Bruce Wayne, sissy playboy. From *The Psychology of Everyday Things:* "My office phone rang. I picked up the receiver and bellowed 'come in' at it."

Today my wife is plodding her way through Western Civilization—some monumentally leaden loaf of a tome—and I'm high over the outermost ozone, neutron-powered and astral, having found my stash of yellowing sci-fi comics from the early fifties: "Lobster Men from Outer Space!," "The Deadly Sirens of Saturn's Rings!" We must be quite the mismatched duo seated on the porch today—her researched facts; my overreaching, supercharged conjectures. It's amazing we don't break off at the hinge and blow away in opposite directions. It's amazing the light, the dense noon light, that strikingly played across Descartes and Margaret Sanger and Hannibal, and also winks off rockets in the void, decides, if "decides" is the word, to hold us, for the moment, in its dispassionate version of parity.

There's a story by Borges, "The Disk." A traveler, claiming to be a king in exile, opens his fist: but nothing's there. Nonetheless, "You may touch it," he says to the narrator. "I felt something cold, and saw a glitter." The strange king says, "It is Odin's disk. It has only one side. In all the world there is nothing else with only one side." By this, we know we're in the land of fable. When my wife and I quietly argue, each of us is one cold, glittering, unswayable side. Yes, but there *are* two of us.

I leave the porch for a short walk. Why do we think of the dead as counselors in our come-and-go confusions? Homer thought so; so does Joe Shmoe. For my purposes today, it's handily misty. Is there a step, a voice? Thousands of people witness Jesus' face in the discolorations of a herring fillet, or Elvis in the gravy stains on a menu. Can't I ask to see my own father for longer than one gray *plink* in the wrist?

There are sensational tales aplenty of parents spookily but confidingly appearing out of the aether, in moments of crisis: "and he helped me land the plane." For me, it isn't like that. In "Warlords of the Microverse!" the fumes from a mysterious elixir shrink our hero, past electrons, to a world—it happens to be, of course, a world of high adventure—in the invisible dye in the fabric of Things As We Know Them, a plane of existence among the neutrinos and tardyons. I hold out my hand, as if I could feel the mist. I suppose if I lived on the level of mist, then I *could* feel it.

By night, we're side by side again in the bed, at peace—Skyler and myself. We're happy more than we're not. She sleeps, and I stroke her hips, I stroke them *hard,* I want to feel the tree of bone inside her body.

We know from physics, though—we're empty air, we're a piffle of elements strung in empty air. She's here and she isn't here.

The tribal plow or deboweler or fish hook: is also "art" on a gallery wall.

A.D. 1250: the women the village calls witches are fallen deeply asleep on the earth floor of a shack, their funky aria of snores is assertable proof of this. They reek of their ritual coating of secret ointment.

They're here; they're flying.

The Division of Reality

A side road gets declared in the history of Western Civilization around the time of Descartes, that rapidly becomes the main freeway of intellectual travel. As it's used, it takes us out of our old universe completely. (A simplification, yes; but a helpful one.)

The world-view of the Middle Ages—mythic, symbolic, its rootedness in cyclical time and in a cosmos of living matter governed by a heedful God—could not control the plagues. "Every technique of this organization of knowledge was used: prayer, ecstatic mysticism, scapegoating, medicine based on sympathetic magic, and so forth. All failed." Then, "under the pressure of its critical problems, Western Europe developed a new way of organizing reality."

This is the Cartesian, the Renaissance, viewpoint. It separates mind from body; objective worlds from subjective; and the parsable realm of nature from the calipers-bearing experimenter. Science as we know it begins. Time becomes a possessable line of small forged logical links. The plagues are finally kept at bay. Now "sanitation" is a concept. Commerce and industry are around the corner, and Newton is waiting there, polishing an apple on his lapel. You can see the sun of a heliocentric universe shining in that redness, blessing the laws of thermodynamics, asking to be squeezed through a prism and compartmented. Everything's bright, yes?

But "the division of reality into a sphere of matter and a sphere of mind provided a very powerful methodology for the study of one and a very inadequate methodology for the study of the other. Our power to manipulate and control the 'outside' world—matter and energy—advanced greatly, but we made no advances in the understanding of our own behavior and our inner experience."

The residua of an older road fare poorly in the new. Cartesian duality says "a thing cannot both be and not be at the same time." And by 1650, the year of Descartes' death, the witches of Europe are having their nipples singed, or worse. We'll eventually fly to the moon, and thereon plant our flag (and whack a golf ball); oh but not before we attempt to eradicate those who meet to wield their broomsticks and fly through their own shadowed minds.

When I think of the splitting road, of the nameable handful of splitting roads the species has followed, I also think of a charming diagram in *Time Warps* by John Gribbin. It shows a filmstrip in which a stick-figure man approaches a chair, considers sitting, but then continues on; and extending from this, and so making the shape of a Y, is another, alternative filmstrip where, at the frame of decision-making, our stick-figure fellow indeed sits down. "The argument put forward so vividly in science fiction and now being increasingly discussed by physicists and mathematicians is that whenever such a choice comes up the entire universe splits in two, and *both* choices 'really' take place, with two separate universes developing as a result."

I like it: this posits a "layerverse" of endless contiguous universes; the ones most near us, horribly boringly like us; and the farther we move in any direction (here, direction's defined as "possibility-sequence") the stronger the malleability, until we'd see (if we *could* see), below the clear light of an afternoon sun, the "*me's*" of ourselves we otherwise only encounter in dream and lunacy. This might *explain* dreams, lunacy, or even something like precognition: "vibrations" from layerverse level X. (It might explain the recognition we feel on viewing Arbus's diverse citizenry.)

But mainly, simply, I'm taken with the integrity this reinvests in each of the nanodecisions of that grand guignol gestalt we call our lives, our daily, our only, lives.

Now I can imagine Nate, our mailman, needing to rest in the shade of the Pest-Kill bug, on this sonofabitchin 103-degree day in Wichita, Kansas. I can see him mop the sting from his eyes, below the outspread plaster wings like ironing boards and the French-horn-like proboscis—at the mercy of every yahoo with a postage stamp. And: will he or won't he gratefully accept the chilled, forbidden beer I'll offer him when he's on the porch? Does he or doesn't he slyly delay the bundle of third-class mail for the substitute's shlepping, tomorrow? Out of each of these, the blossoming of two cosmoses, two futures.

In the sci-fi newspaper comic strip *Twin Earths* (which started its rather successful run in 1952) we're introduced to Terra, "a planet identical to our own in size and appearance" but traveling the sky in our orbit, at our speed, on the *opposite* side of the sun—and so forever unknown, or at least unknown until one of its agents contacts Garry Verth of our FBI. Terra is 92% female, and most glamorously so, as drawn by artist Al McWilliams. In 1903 (Earth year) the Terran femmes developed flying saucers, and . . . well, many *and*'s, much atom-blaster mellerdrama.

I can't say it's *distinguished* writing, but I'll suggest it serves well as an emblem (much of comicdom does) for some of the twofold pleasures and afflictions that define us. So when Wallace Stevens writes of "Bonnie and Josie . . . / Celebrating the marriage / Of flesh and air," he's established his own binary planets. I think of Terra and Earth as the astrological influences over Katherine and Jessica Goddeke—twins, but born in different years, a span of minutes on either side of the first of January 1992.

John Casti claims that, if a signal received from outer space "shows that there is a 'second Earth' out there where extraterrestrials worry about the stock market crashes, go on vacations to 'Hawaii,' and play baseball, then the message would probably result in a vast, almost unbelievable disappointment." I'm not sure about that.

I am sure Neely's bringing her jillion-dollar grin and beating tomtom derriere into Daddy Zach's, an after-hours jazz club where her boyfriend jams piano in a five-guy group called Protoplasm.

He loves it, up there. He loves it especially when she's in the audience, wearied out from jiggledancing, lost now in a replenishing cloud of his burning playing. The keyboard responds to his fingers like an animal being stroked, the music glimmers off into the stratosphere—and, after a day of Post Office labor, he's all of a sudden phantasmal and pure. "Yeah! Nate, the Piano Potentate!" the emcee says. "Let's hear it!" After a day of dull delivery, the music carries him—*he's* delivered.

Later still, they're asleep together, his hand as black as anthracite on one buttery cheek of her rump.

A Forum

Until she was seven, she was in the care of "Mamselle," a French nanny. Once, they passed a tin-shack bumtown built in the bed of a dried-up reservoir. "This was a potent memory: seeing the other side of the tracks, holding the hand of one's governess." She had asked, even then—but had been refused—to clamber down and investigate. She was unflappable. She itched to touch the face inside a face. "She once confided that she envied a girlfriend who'd been raped. She wanted to have that punishing, degrading experience, too." Where could she find prisoners condemned to die? Streetwalkers? "She never looked away, which took courage and independence." She said, "If you're born one thing, you can dare to be ten thousand other things."

Some days she'd leave at dusk—"she seemed to be more alive in the dark"—and walk all night: the subway corridors, the bus station urinals, anywhere extremity set up camp, or a wayward tenderness flourished in rubbish. Blending in. Becoming habitual. Turning the furtive peek into a stakeout. There are contact sheets over years, in which you can follow her gradual progress "from the street to their home to their living room to their bedroom—like a narrative, a process leading up to some strange intimacy."

The razor blades didn't send her away. She'd stand in the steam of a sewer grating like some corner's resident dybbuk. And she'd stalk for long past the first weak spasms of dawn, until maybe seven A.M., in hopes of something transcendent in the day's as-yet-untainted light—"a fat lady in a Santa Claus outfit somersaulting heavily down a grassy hill; a solitary young man, totally nude, raising his arms to the sky."

These, this, she photographed:

The American Nazi Party. Presto the Fire Eater. Russian midget Gregory Ratoucheff. Morales the Mexican dwarf. The eight-foot "Jewish Giant" Eddie Carmel. Child hookers working the piss-scent alleys of Rome. The Human Pincushion. Sealo the Seal Boy (his hands grew out of his shoulders). "A big black lady who wandered around the beach, calling herself God." Charlotte Moorman the stripper cellist. Potato Chip Manzini. "When we were breeding our dogs, Diane took pictures of animals copulating." Congo the Jungle Creep. Fortune tellers. Mob chauffeurs. In the

Hades-like mist of the Monroe Street Ukrainian Baths she secretly shot, as her ladyfriend Cheech said, "wrinkled old crones with hanging boobs." Miss Stormé de Larverie, "male impersonator." Lady Olga the Bearded Wonder. The desk clerk at a transvestite hotel. Bondage parlors (a leather-booted mistress is dripping hot wax on a naked, kneeling penitent). Prince Robert de Rohan Courtney, author of over 9,000 poems in a private doggerel language, who lived in a 6-by-9-foot room he called "the Jade Tower" and claimed being heir "to the throne of the Byzantine Roman Empire." Epidermal artiste Jack Dracula, he of 306 tattoos (28 stars on his face alone, around a fancy pair of trompe l'oeil goggles). The pet crematorium. Many dozens of nudists. Harelips. Gimps. An orgy in a New Jersey motel ("where everybody sat around eating peanut butter on crackers before they fucked," she said). The Important Order of Red Men, shoestore salesmen and plumbers and druggists who "dressed up in Indian feathers and brandished sequined tomahawks." Slaughterhouses, issuing their unthinkable, tissuey rivers. Vicki Strasberg, a transvestite whore. A lovely, gypsy-bloused albino sword swallower ("her arms are stretched out like Christ on the cross, but her head is thrown back triumphantly"). A New Jersey housewife cradling her pet macaque, in an unintentional faux-pietà scene. A pec-oiled bodybuilder proudly displaying his three-foot trophy in a shabby backstage room. The weazened. The deformedly luscious. Hunchbacks. Glitz-trip party girls on a wine-damaged mattress the morning after. Moondog, blind, in his Viking helmet decorated with tusks, the only maestro of the "oo" and the "uni"—"percussion instruments of his own design." A group of middle-aged retardates at a home in Vineland, New Jersey—"these people are so angelic," she said, and made her Pentax a recognized fixture amongst them over several visits: the faces are so distorted they nearly seem to blur at their perimeters, as if nature gave up on precision here, heads sifting into a passing laugh or an eerie yelping, planets clouded unfathomably at their poles, and Earth isn't spoken here.

"Such a gallery of the pitiful and grotesque in close-up has never before been seen," somebody said—it was a contemporary of Leonardo da Vinci's, passing judgment on his sketches of the human parade.

She didn't invent these people; she found them, she gave them a forum.

She also recorded a Boy Scout meeting. Tricia Nixon's wedding. Coretta King. A police academy. Ozzie and Harriet. Borges. Gloria Vanderbilt's baby boy. The Metropolitan Opera. The DAR. She wanted a range, she explained, "both posh and sordid"—"all posed," her biographer says, "in the same grave, troubling manner." *This* explains the retracted assignments, the canceled bookings, the spit. We don't want to be reminded.

Anubis's head is sleek, designed entirely of sly energy tapering into a long-jawed angle. Anubis: the Jackal-headed god. He parts the darkness of the tomb itself with that friction-resistant snout.

Horus the Falcon-headed god. And Thoth, the god of scribes, with the head of an Ibis: its elegantly attenuating stylus-like beak. The goddess Sekhmet, Lion-headed. Pasht, Cat-headed (from her, our word *puss*). Hathor, with the generously bulbous head of a Cow. More so, the Hippopotamus head of pregnant Taheret . . .

The whole zoöcapita pantheon. When I was a child I sometimes toyed with the cartoon notion of lifting them like bottles of oil-and-vinegar dressing, and shaking until the sections were marbled-together unseparatably.

This is the fear: that hackles erect, that sex is nested hairily in a crevice, that we carry relict canine teeth, and whatever might seem deific in us comes laced with the touch of the beast.

"Both worlds seemed as one to her."

Trying to put her face on, for a breath's space—could it fit me? Would her foreign nerves link meaningfully to my brambled-up receptors? or dangle like color-coded wires from a broken phone?

Hello? *Hello?*

The Other Side

And Angela of Foligno "was a wealthy, weak, immoral woman"—no details are provided, I'm sorry to say, though they're enjoyable to imagine. And Andrew Corsini: "the most immoral youth in Florence." And Torello da Poppi: "led a diabolical life." And Mary of Egypt: "was, beginning at twelve and for seventeen years thereafter, a prostitute." The list of male-factors who become Saints in the Church is long and strangely persuasive of sudden aboutface turnings in the moral course of certain people's lives. For instance Hubert of Tongres, "a fierce immoral man" who "was con-verted by a white stag." Having brought it to bay, he listened to it speak ("or to a voice out of the leaves"); it sent him to Bishop St. Lambert of Maestricht for religious instruction.

I'm also fond of a story Evelyn Waugh tells, of a night in 1929 in the Sudanese brothel quarter of Port Said. He and his friends are dragged (he *says* they're "dragged") by "three girls in bedraggled dress" to a house with *Maison Dorée* painted over its door. But neither the women nor the atmosphere is appealing, and Waugh and his party leave, to further wander the district. "On our way back we came upon another gaily illuminated building called *Maison Chabanais*. We went in, and were surprised to en-counter Madame and all her young ladies from the *Maison Dorée*. It was, in fact, her back door. Sometimes, she explained, gentlemen went away unsatisfied, determined to find another house, then as often as not they found the way round to the other side, and the less observant ones never discovered their mistake."

I was thinking of this, of all this, as I looked at an Arbus photograph, a landscape of a tree-lined lake. It's spring. The water is shirred by the breeze. There's so much light, the farther trees seem candied in it. Then the hills, and the sky.

But when you look to the bottom, you see the electrical outlet, covered by water and grass. It's a photograph *of* a photograph that's a lobby mural. Nothing is one thing. Simple truths.

I was looking until the season changed, and the trees were cased in a lilac-tinted ice. The snow came up to my ankles. The tired light was winter light, its touch on the frozen water trembled. Wind rose, like a thin voice in the branches. It was winter, and a winter bird dropped down the sky as if it were scratching designs in crystal. A voice in the branches—I kept on walking. It darkened, and I kept on walking, the sky grew deep in stars, the night was close, and it whispered, then quieted.

It was winter, and he was calling me.

Note

I rely on Patricia Bosworth's excellent biography *Diane Arbus,* and on the monographs of Diane Arbus's work from *Aperture* and *Picture Magazine.* Also consulted have been *Purity and Danger* (Mary Douglas); *The Two and the One* (Mircea Eliade); *Masks of the Universe* (Edward Harrison); *The Reenchantment of the World* (Morris Berman); *Time Warps* (John Gribbin); *Einstein's Space & Van Gogh's Sky* (Lawrence Leshan and Henry Margenau); *Paradigms Lost* (John L. Casti). Quoted material is sometimes altered for purposes of rhythm, concision, collage.

Albert Goldbarth is Distinguished Professor of Humanities at Wichita State University and the author of numerous collections of prize-winning poetry, including *Popular Culture, Arts & Sciences,* and the winner of the National Book Critics Circle Award, *Heaven and Earth* (Georgia, 1991). He is also the author of a collection of essays, *A Sympathy of Souls.*